CRICUT • THE BIBLE

[12 BOOKS IN 1]

The Definitive Guide to Master All Machines With Projects From Beginners to Advanced to Spoil Family and Friends and Start Your Business

By

Molly Hale

Disclaimer

This book's content is solely intended for general informative purposes. Although every attempt has been made to guarantee that the material is correct and current, the author disclaims all explicit and implied warranties and representations on the availability, correctness, appropriateness, completeness, and reliability of the information provided herein. You bear full responsibility for any reliance you may have on such material.

Any loss, harm, claim, liability, or damage of any kind originating from, arising out of, or connected in any manner to any mistakes or omissions in this book—including but not limited to inaccuracies or typographical errors—is expressly disclaimed by the author. Additionally, the author disclaims all obligation for any loss, harm, claim, liability, or damage of any kind arising from the use of this book's contents.

It is the reader's obligation to use good judgment and, if needed, seek advice from qualified experts before starting any crochet projects or activities that are included in this book. Any actions or decisions the reader takes as a result of using the material in this book are not the author's responsibility.

Table of Contents

INTRODUCTION

Cricuts are electronic cutting machines used for a wide variety of craft projects, including but not limited to paper crafts like scrapbooking and card making. The Cricut's only limitation is the user's own creativity. There are Cricut cartridges available for the machines. This new tool's rotating cutter allows it to cut intricate patterns and symbols from a variety of printing techniques as well as provide a precise, effective, quick, and simple touch. Modern Cricuts are still capable of amazing things with paper, but they can do much more. You have more artistic freedom than ever before with the machine and tools of the Cricut machine, and you can choose from a huge selection of tool attachments for your Cricut to use with a wide variety of materials. Due to its ease of use and effectiveness for both lovers and artists, this device is important. Cricut devices come in a plethora of varieties; they support a wide range of layouts and function with different textures.

Cricut's machines are fundamentally extremely fantastic printers. They are functional die cutters and artistic planners that assist you in creating enjoyable designs for various projects you wish to undertake.

There are many different models available, and you can pick from a variety of exceptional varieties. In the Explore series of devices, there is a feature called Cricut Design Space that allows you to put anything you want to build in space and then print it. If you're tired of looking at the same photos every day or if you want to cut out a pattern in vinyl without getting frustrated, a Cricut machine might be a great help.

Cricut is multipurpose, the versatility is unlimited. Cricut makes complex paper crafts, personalized home decor, and trendy clothes. Hobbyists and professionals utilize it to explore artistic paths due to its adaptability.

Beginning crafting can be intimidating, especially for beginners. Not to worry! The Cricut community offers classes, workshops, and online tools for all crafters. You can learn vinyl cutting, 3D paper crafts, or improve in the community. These Cricut crafting classes, typically by experts, can teach beginners.

Beyond personal creativity, Cricut has transformed small businesses and ambitious entrepreneurs. Entrepreneurs can delve into the personalized goods, stationery, and event décor world. The Exciting World of Cricut has helped crafters start profitable companies. We can't ignore the world's continual creativity as we explore the colorful Cricut community. New materials, equipment, and software expand possibilities daily.

Cricut's future promises advancement and transformation, boosting creativity and ingenuity.

Cricut Adaptive Tool System

The Quick Swap Housing System, which is exclusive to the Cricut Maker, allows you to switch out razors without having to modify the housing. The Cricut Maker Adaptive Tool Switch System is also unique. Building multi-dimensional designs is not only made easier by this, but it also makes them more practical. As long as you possess one instrument with the housing, you can only obtain its other blades and points. The average cost of housing plus tips is $44.99–$49.99; however, you can buy just the pointers for $24.99–$29.99.

The Wavy Blade

The wavy blade adds a new meaning to designs. For gift tags or bags, envelopes, invitations, paper flowers, and much more, you can add a whimsical touch to practically any content.

Things to Keep in Mind Whenever You Use the Wavy Blade:

This blade resembles a revolving blade with real tiny models and sharp corners. Making sure the cut is at least 3⁄4 percent is the best course of action. Every cut is unique, and the Maker has no way of knowing where the waves will even cut. When you switch it to WAVY, you'll see the word WAVY below the periodic cut line that you initially saw in Design Space.

Utilizable parts

- Acryl Acetate
- Paper Crepe
- The Fabric
- Vinyl and Iron-On Vinyl
- The Felt
- Paper
- Cardstock
- Perforation Blade

Perfectly separated puncture cuts are made possible by the perforation blade. It makes it simpler to create and use things like raffle tickets, countdown calendars, tear-off project sheets, and more. The perforation cuts allow you to break off instantly without having to fold beforehand, and the cuts are neat and smooth.

Debossing Tip

This tip might be the most exciting if you were disappointed to see that the Cricut Cuttlebug is no longer available. The debossing tip can be used to apply elegant black anodized versions to invitations, envelopes, home decor projects, and more. Unlike directories with an embossing/engraving device, you will choose the desired location and emboss the label to create a completely unique and different design.
it can be used with the following materials:

- Cardstock
- Faux Leather or Leather
- Message Board
- Kraft Paper
- Paper
- Basswood

Engraving Tip

We are aware that a lot of Cricut crafters have been waiting for it for a very long time! A tool that engraves designs onto fragile surfaces without breaking or causing harm. In fact, the engraving tip is already here! Monograms, patterns, embellishments, and more can be engraved on even the most fragile materials, such as acrylic and aluminum.
it can be used With the following:

- Cricut Metal Sheet
- Aluminum
- Acrylic
- Cricut Ink Cartridges

Essentially, the heart of a Cricut cutting-edge machine consists of cartridges, which are inserted into the cutter system to create any desired layout on a piece of paper.
There is a large variety of cartridges available on the market globally, but not all of these cartridges are compatible with all types of machines. One essential component that allows musicians and crafters to make a wide variety of designs in beautiful colors and styles is the Cricut cartridge, which works exclusively with Cricut machines.
A variety of cartridges with more packages to choose from than previous ones have been introduced recently due to changes in printing technologies. Ink cartridges are utilized in inkjet printers, whereas laser cartridges are utilized in laser printers. These two types of printer cartridges are the most common ones available. They continue to use ink-jet printers in all Cricut machines.

Initially, Cricut ink cartridges were only available in black; however, a few other colors were eventually released. Subsequently, as printing technology advanced, ink cartridges were developed, and efforts were made to offer various font styles, layouts, and colors for contour formation.

Using various and unique types of cartridges that enable users to create cut and creative designs in nearly any font, layout, color, and style is essential to the success of this Cricut system.

Shape cartridge: it comes in a variety of shapes, such as newsprint dolls, animals, sports, boxes, tags, and bags.

Licensed cartridge: This lets users get the cut made with their favorite characters, like Disney's Mickey Mouse, Hello Kitty, Toy Story from Pixar, and more.

Classmate cartridge: as its name suggests, it was designed specifically for use in classrooms. This includes typefaces, shapes, and layouts; it also includes a visual analysis tool and teacher ideas and expressions.

Solutions cartridge: cheaper than rest. The shapes include campouts, baseball, soccer, welding, and more.

As was already established, the extensive selection of Cricut cartridges gives crafters—especially younger customers—the chance to try out their artistic abilities without the use of a computer. On the other hand, they can easily create designs in various shapes and colors with the Cricut ink cartridge.

BOOK 1:
CHOOSING THE BEST CRICUT MACHINE

To choose the ideal machine for your crafting needs, it's crucial to consider all of your options before you buy your first Cricut. First, you must restock on necessities like photo capsules and Cricut ribbon. These capsules can be customized with various themes to highlight and honor any occasion, including upcoming events, holidays, and special occasions. A large quantity of colored paper and a pad to reduce that contrast with the size of your system are also necessary.

For each machine, there will be a brief introduction, then go into further detail regarding its features and conclude this piece with some advice on selecting a machine. So, let's get started

Explore Air 2

One of Cricut's more traditional machines, the Explore Air 2, is still a very good option. It cuts more than 100 materials, has a base price of $249.99, and is available in various colors. The Explore Air 2 has tools for scoring, writing, and cutting.

Cricut Explore Air 2 Unboxing

With more than a hundred different materials, this Cricut can cut, sketch, and do so much more. Cutting is quick thanks to wireless cutting, cloud-based templates, and automated cut adjustments. It also has a great selection of accessories for precise, accurate cuts.

The Cricut Explore Air 2 was introduced in the middle of 2016, and it is packed with features that made it the fastest and most adaptable cutter available. It was a long-lasting favorite among crafters and quickly sold out. It has significantly decreased in price over time and is currently one of the best prices on a home vinyl cutter you can find. We frequently get asked this question when discussing cutting machines: Since Explore Air and Explore Air 2 seem to have all the same features and virtually identical looks.

What is the difference? Speed and color are the answer. In the Explore Air 2, there is a 2x quick mode that deals with cardstock, vinyl, and iron-on. In addition, it comes in three gorgeous hues: sky blue, mint green, and pastel pink. Now let's have a look inside. Your package should include the following items, at the very least:

- A training manual.
- Carving pad made by Cricut.
- Blade for cutting (pre-installed).
- Cricut Explore Air 2 (if you skipped this one, the box was fairly light).

- USB power + cords.
- Silver pen and connector adapter.
- Cardstock plus vinyl samples (we've read about a few unfinished kits).

We'll talk about the key features of Explore Air 2, some of which are really cool. You may use the fine-point blade, deep-point blade, and bonded leather blade as three different cutting tools in the Explore Air 2. With these materials, you may cut more than a dozen different types of substance, such as:

- Chipboard material.
- phony.
- Sheets of foam.
- fabrics bonded.
- Document.
- Print and vinyl, chipboard and foam panels, and bonded textiles.
- Packaged Smart Dial

With this dial, you can easily pick the substance to cut, and the Cricut will take care of determining the right cutting depth and speed for you. You'll save a ton of time and content by doing this, which takes a lot of the headache and guesswork out of choosing the cut settings.

2x Fast Mode
Circuit's Explore Air 2 has a 2x quick mode that doubles the speed at which you can cut thin materials like cardstock, vinyl, and paper. Another major time-saver, since cutting certain tasks can take an unexpectedly long time!

Accessories
Even some lovely attachments can be used with the device. You can use the scoring stylus to make 3D paper art or offer your handmade cards a smooth appearance. Each of these tools may be used simultaneously because the Explore Air 2 has a dual tool holder. This ensures that you can cut and draw or cut and score in a single move without having to switch instruments.

Software for Cricut Design Space
Cricut Design Space software and its free design application are used with the Explore Air 2. Because the software is cloud-based, you can view and operate your projects on

your computer, machine, or mobile device with ease. You can submit the models to be sliced wirelessly because the unit even has Bluetooth built in.

These are the five primary features of the Cricut Explore Air 2:
- Cut five different accessories for carving, scoring, and scoring, as well as more than 100 different styles of products.
- For different material types, the Smart Set Dial automatically adjusts the cut depth and speed.
- Quick mode splits into two.
- To draw and cut or cut and rate, use a double tool holder.
- Cloud-based development and wireless cutting are interdependent.

Pros and Cons of the Cricut Air Explorer 2
- Bluetooth cutting that is wireless.
- substantial community support.
- Free SVGs may be imported.
- Precision cuts on vinyl and cardstock.
- Equipped with a smart set dial, quick cutting, double tool keeper, and two swift modes.
- Wonderfully constructed device.

Cons:
- Not a touchscreen.
- Not the strongest for cutting large bulky fabrics or cloth.
- Cricut Design Room is a basic and frequently unusable tool.
- Strict cutting dimensions (12" by 24").
- Internet access on PCs and Macs is part of the web-based functionality.
- Pace, Flexibility, and Precision in Cutting

When purchasing a new art cutter, the most important thing to remember is how good it slices. Cricut machines really shine in this place because they are faster and more efficient cutters than any other home appliance. The Explore Air 2 cuts more smoothly than any other home cutter we have tested in this price range, though it still can't compete with the more expensive Cricut Maker.

Because it is accurate, strong, and adaptable, the Explore Air 2 is an excellent cutter for a variety of home ventures. It can precisely cut through even the most complex prototypes and is flexible enough to cut through more than a hundred different materials. You can use the accessory connector and cut and sketch at the same time with colorful Cricut pens.

Compared to the original Explore Air Cricut, the Explore Air 2 even slices twice as easily. This ensures that it is among the best devices you can buy for your design requirements. Circuit's Explore Air 2 is one of our favorite cutters because it has consistently shown that it can cut through even the most conventional craft materials. All you have to do is set the content form on the Smart Set dial to ensure that the unit is ready to cut precisely and cleanly.

The unit comes with a high-quality fine-point blade made of German carbide steel. It offers precision cuts because it is stronger and more finely tuned than most cutting blades over an extended period of use. However, when the cuts start to become less precise, one of the first things you should do is think about replacing the blade with a new one.

Additionally, the Explore Air 2 includes an extension connector that can hold the scoring stylus or a variety of Cricut pen colors. To create unique and lovely cards or photo albums, you will sketch, compose, and score using these resources. You can cut and sketch or cut and score at the same time thanks to the Cricut's dual tool holder. This ensures that you won't need to change tools or confirm your pass parameters, which is a significant time saver.

It's a little noisy, which is the key down side of the Explore Air 2. You will be informed of this every time you try to make a phone call while completing a job, even though it applies to all vinyl cutters. You can't hold an eye on the device if it's not visible in the back ground!

The Explore Air 2 offers accurate, simple cuts when cutting most materials, though. Because of the dual tool holder's added versatility, By utilizing your skills, you can accomplish a greater variety of tasks with ease.

A wide variety of materials can be sliced by the Cricut Explore Air 2: over a hundred different styles! Breaks using three distinct blades, encompassing over a thousand different products! The majority of light to medium-weight objects can be cut with the fine-point blade, which is meant for the most challenging cuts. Examples of such items are:

- Cardstock
- Adhesive vinyl.
- Paper with a Textured Surface.
- printer paper.
- Copy board.
- Vinyl Iron-On (also known as Heat Transfer Vinyl or HTV).
- Paper

Additionally, the Explore Air 2 allows you to remove thicker materials (up to 1.5 thick (mm). Even though the fine-point blade cuts at a 45-degree angle, you could treat tougher materials like: by purchasing the additional Deep-Point blade + housing (does not include) and cutting at a 60-degree angle.

- Fiberboard.
- sheets of foam.
- Material for stamps.
- heavy cardstock.
- Magnet.
- Chipboard material.

However, the Bonded-Fabric blade (which is not included) can also be used by the Explore Air 2 to cut fused fabric, allowing you to draw and cut appliques and quilting squares. Moreover, you can use the Washable Fabric Markers to simultaneously cut and circle your fabric pieces. Be aware that in order to cut through many fabrics heavier than vinyl and medium-weight paper forms, you will need to purchase these additional blades.

If you want to cut with a lot more flexibility, cut through tougher fabrics, or handle cloth more neatly, your best option is to look at the more expensive (and newest) Cricut type. It will accomplish everything that Explore Air 2 is unable to.

Twice as Fast as the First Cricut Air Explore in Cutting

The Cricut Explore Air 2 is a speedy cutter that can cut up to twice as quickly as the original model. This is the main technical difference between the two versions, and it will ultimately save you a lot of time.

Vinyl, iron-on, most paper forms, and cardstock are all lightweight materials that the unit deals with in its 2x rapid mode. It will cut these thin materials at double the speed of the standard setting. This is great when you need to create a large number of invitations or stickers to send out, but it also helps save time on individual tasks.

However, there are a few drawbacks to the 2x quick mode. Not all designs and materials are suitable for the 2x rapid mode. When you pick the substance environment, you'll see if the material is too dense for quick cutting. In the slower environment, any relatively complex patterns can be.

More accurately sliced. More noise is produced in the quick mode than in the regular velocity. As the system gets louder, the noise levels also pick up.

All things considered, this quick mode is a fantastic new feature that cuts through vinyl and paper, the two most common materials you'll come across.

Design: Stylish and Well-Made Machine

Our favorite thing about the Cricut devices is how beautifully they are designed. Both their beauty and ease of use seem to be present in them. This also applies to the Air 2 Explorer! You would absolutely adore how the machine looks when it is lying on your desk and how simple it is to obtain a cut.

The Cricut Explore Air 2 appears to have been designed by people who appreciate aesthetics. It has an elegant, curved design and is available in an ever-expanding spectrum of colors.

In examining a machine's architecture, we also consider its user interface and auditory characteristics. The Explore Air 2 is packed with useful features that make it quick, stable, and simple to use.

Packed with Practical and Simple Features

The Explore Air 2 is incredibly easy to operate thanks to its many features. It opens instantly with a single button press. The intelligent set dial smoothly rotates to pick your content, determining the depth and cut pace on its own. The double tool holder allows you to cut and sketch or cut and emboss in a single run. The 2x quick mode ensures that you will spend less time monitoring and waiting for the system to finish your tasks.

The Explore Air 2 is missing a touchscreen, among other items. Rather, the cutting software monitor and the dial are all on your phone or device. Explore Air 2 is made simpler to use by both of these features. Cricut included so many useful features that real crafters would find useful. The people who have their computers built can be identified.

Cricut Design Space

A lot of crafters spend a lot of time using design software, either customizing installed templates or starting from scratch with new projects. In any case, it is important to comprehend the simple workings of the design tools so that you can construct precisely what you want.

Cricut Design Room is a free program that can be used with any Cricut system. The simplest cutting, painting, and scoring styles can be designed by it.

Some people believe that using Design Space is difficult. You can turn to a ton of online tutorials for help with the Cricut culture. Some would argue that the Design Room is overly simplistic given their design objectives. To give to your cutter later, you can thankfully upload SVGs created in other applications or with Design Room that you install.

Bluetooth Enabled for Wireless Cutting

The Cricut Explore Air 2 has Bluetooth integrated into it. This indicates that it is set up for wireless cutting right out of the package. (Examine Air's "Air"!) The original Cricut Explore required the purchase and assembly of a specific connector in order to be wired to Bluetooth and cut wirelessly. If you'd like, you can still use the included USB cable to connect to your device.

Fantastic Online Community

You gain access to Cricut's fantastic online community, which is the most valuable benefit of purchasing a Cricut from them. Although their cutters are fairly simple to operate, you may, of course, encounter problems and need help with troubleshooting.

Various Machine Components

- A tool cup to hold scissors, pens, and other implements.
- Clamp accessory A. This is where the accessory connector comes pre-installed. Add a pen to draw with instead of cutting. For carrying scoring blades, it's also good.
- Sword clamp B. The blade is included in the package. Whether you need to cut vinyl pieces or replace it, this is where you want to go.
- Compartments for storing accessories. The Explore Air 2 has two storage pockets in addition to the tool cup. The smaller pocket on the left is carried by knives, extra blade housings, and the extension connector. It has a magnetic strip to hold replacement blades firmly in place and prevent them from spinning. The larger compartment is great for holding longer tools or pens.
- Dial for Smart Set. Turn the dial to pick the item that will be cut. It feels good to transform and indicates which materials you should cut with the 2x quick mode.
- Cutting Board. This is the amount of content that would be put into our Cricut machine. Our content is sticky on the one hand to ensure that it stays firmly in place.

Just a brief note regarding the accessory and blade clamps: in the unlikely event that you need to remove the blade or accessory clip, simply pull open the lever and remove the metal housing. The blade rests on the inside, and there's a tiny plunger on the end. For the blade that is magnetically holding out, you should press down on this. If you still want to change the blade, simply remove it and drop another one in. To use a pen, simply unlock accessory clamp A, drop it in, and close the clamp.

Cricut Explore 3

The Cricut Explore 3 is coming next! I've had a good amount of experience working with mine. Given the number three in the machine's name, you could assume that this is just a more advanced model of the Cricut Explore Air 2. And it really is, to be honest. That being said, you are not required to obtain it.

Both of these machines are still being promoted by Cricut and may be bought from their website. Also, the Explore 3 is still more expensive than the Cricut Explore Air 2. What benefits do you receive for spending a little more money, then?

The base price of the Explore 3 is $319, and it can cut through more than 100 materials and utilize tools for scoring, cutting, and writing. Additionally, print-then-cut was supported. So far, it sounds similar to the Explore Air 2, just more pricey. What then is different? Because it uses Smart Materials, it can cut up to 12 feet rather than just 2. it also runs smoother and faster than the Explore Air 2.

What can be cut with the Cricut Explore 3?

I won't go into too much detail about the materials and tools this machine can cut because its capabilities are very similar to those of the Explore Air 2. When utilizing Smart Materials, the Cricut Explore 2 may be used without a mat, which is a significant difference.

And with some of those Smart Materials, it can also make really long cuts. The maximum cut sizes for a single cut are as follows:

- Vinyl: 29.7 cm x 3.6 m (11.7 in x 12 feet)
- Iron-On: 29.7 cm x 1.2 m (11.7 in x 4 ft)
- 11.7 in × 11.2 in (29.7 cm x 28.4 cm) paper

Not needing a mat is a great plus. It saves time to just load the material and hit the enter key. It's also unnecessary to keep buying mats and attempting to use them when they near death and lose their stick.

There's also faster cutting with the Cricut Explore 3. while compared to the Explore Air 2's fast mode, it is twice as quick while cutting Smart Materials.

So, do you think it was all worth it? What you want to make with your machine will determine that! If you're interested in utilizing Smart Materials without a mat, the Explore 3 is well worth the additional cost. And don't worry, you can still use different materials to cut with a mat.

Making lengthy or repetitive cuts can possibly be something you enjoy doing. Let's say you wish to cut out a gazillion little decals. Simply load a roll of Smart Vinyl, then step back and let the machine work its magic. Replace the mats and don't start the cut over.

Cricut Maker

It is a true powerhouse in terms of weight and do-it-yourself capability. The Cricut Explore Air 2 and this one are nearly identical in size and appearance, but they are very different inside!

For the most dedicated crafters among us, this machine is quite amazing. It cuts more than 300 materials and has a base price of $299. Comparatively, the Explore Air 2 and Explore 3 cut through more than 100 materials.

In addition, the Maker uses more than eleven tools for engraving, debossing, writing, scoring, and cutting. Its maximum material length and width, however, are the same as those of the Explore Air 2 at two feet and twelve inches, respectively. It also has print-then-cut capabilities.

What materials can you cut using the Cricut Maker?

The Maker's ability to cut a wide variety of materials is actually its main selling point. It cuts everything that the Explore Air 2 can cut, plus more with its speciality blades, including leather, thicker chipboard, corrugated cardboard, wood veneer, bass/balsa wood, and more. It is compatible with the foil transfer kit, writes, and scores much like the Air 2.

Let's discuss the differences now. This machine is simply more powerful all around. Its commercial-grade technology likely explains why it weighs significantly more since it features an adaptive tool system that increases cutting power by ten times by controlling the blades and cut pressure. The superior fine-point blade found on the Explore Air 2 is also used for simple cutting.

Unique tools and blades used by the Maker

Numerous tools are available for cutting, writing, scoring, debossing, engraving, and other tasks at The Maker. The Maker has an excellent knife blade in addition to the fine-point blade. Cutting up to 2.4mm (3/32") materials, the knife blade elevates the deep point cutting of the Explore Air 2.

Among other things, you cut balsa and basswood with the knife blade.

Sewing enthusiasts will also find The Maker to be a great resource. In the early stages of the epidemic, I made some masks at home using my Maker and rotary blade, though I haven't utilized the sewing feature very much yet.

The Maker's rotary blade not only creates extremely accurate cuts, but it can also imprint designs on fabric. Additionally, you may purchase tools for creating wavy lines, scoring, perforating, debossing, engraving, and scoring. The engraving and debossing blades works well.

Cricut Maker 3

The Maker 3 will be our fourth machine to profile. The only machine that I have never owned or tried myself is this one. However, it was released during the same time that Cricut released the Explore 3, so I am very familiar with its features.

What can you cut with the Cricut Maker 3?
The Maker 3 performs all of the functions of the original Maker machine, but it also has the same enhancements as the Explore 3.
- If you use Smart Materials, you don't need a cutting mat to make cuts.
- If you use Smart Materials, the length can expand significantly—up to 12 feet.
- For large or lengthy projects, it is compatible with the roll holder (available separately).
- Compared to the Cricut Maker, it cuts twice as fast.

The starting price is $429. Thus, the Cricut Maker 3 can be an excellent option if you want access to all of the quick change tools, the knife blade, and the extra benefits of longer, faster cuts on Smart Materials.

Cricut Maker vs. Explore: A Comparison

You don't have to update right away if you already own an Explore Air 2. It's similar to when the next iPhone is released; while you might be enticed by all the exciting new features, the current model always functions flawlessly. The Cricut would not stop assisting while using the current device, so update if you like the best and newest features, but don't think it's necessary.

We will, however, accept that Cricut has made the most sophisticated version, and since you adore it, you won't miss it when you can afford it. If you've been worrying about updating, now is the time to begin planning an update because the manufacturer has been offering discounts since it was first launched.

What's New in the Cricut Maker? What Does It Have That the Explore Does Not?
You won't miss it if you can afford it, but we will accept that Cricut has made the most sophisticated version. It's time to begin planning an update if you've been worrying

about updating because the Manufacturer is now starting to offer sales since it was first launched. Compared to the Explore Air 2, it features a rotating blade that cuts and styles fabric more effectively! Since this is unquestionably the Cricut machine's legend and a fantastic advancement over earlier models. You'll be amazed every time at how well the rotary blade trims hard materials like felt and cloth. You also never had a texture before because, on Air 2, your texture has always been difficult to work with and produced equivocal results. Now that you have this Maker, you can trim the best materials! To be clear, the Explore Air 2's ability to cut the cloth always needs a backing and a blade stabilizer like Warm Air n' Bond added to the cloth when matting is ineffective because the blade begins to pull on the cloth but does not make neat cuts like a spinning rotary machine.

Additionally, you can use patterned or colorful material for "Print and Cut." Will that change your life? Never, never. Nice to have it? You can print a design like Happy Valentine's Day by using a template on a sweetheart paper, then cut around the template. This is exactly how I'm thinking about doing it. It's great that you don't have to waste ink on printing white paper back to back.

With 10x more strength and a stronger (above 2.44 mm thinner) coating, the knife blade helps you trim. You must purchase a Manufacturer if you wish to cut wood using your cutting machine.

Tool System that is Simple and Extendable

This unique word basically suggests that the Creator was made to grow alongside a craftsman and match a wide range of new resources that the Cri cut machine has on hand. There are rumors that they are discussing producing over forty distinct types of blades. Therefore, choose the maker if it bothers you that you can't use the recently launched cutters and attachments.

The Cricut Maker's External Design

Helps you charge and display your phone or iPad while you're designing with the charging port and device monitor holder.

increased device capacity. In addition, the Maker features a larger storage cabinet and two storage cups.

Choose the material type without using the smart dial. To start, when you set up a cut-out pattern, you can quickly make some material adjustments from your screen. In addition, it teaches you about using a variety of customized products rather than just those that match the smart dial. The machine lacks a cartridge port. If you are a long-time customer of the Cricut machine and you have an older machine cartridge, you will need to purchase an adapter in order to use these with the Manufacturer. When dealing with new users who have never owned a Cricut, you don't even consider this.

Which Is Right for You?

Cricut Maker

One of the best cutting machines is the Cricut Maker. Although it has been completely redesigned, it seems to be similar to the Discover machine line. It has extra features in addition to doing everything that Cricut Explore can. You shouldn't need a stabilizer like the Cricut Explore line because Cricut Creator cuts unbound cloth using a tiny Rotary Cutter. If you're trying to make felt crafts, this unit is for you because it often makes you smile wonderfully. With the Knife cutter, Cri Cut Maker frequently removes thicker items (up to 3/32"), such as balsa wood and soft leather. Using Score Circle, it will give each type of material a rating. The Adaptive Kit for Cricut Maker was designed to use materials that Cricut hasn't even thought of yet! They have a few more resources to test, so when more features are released, this machine will be able to do more. On the Cricut line, the price point of $399, which is frequently on sale for $349, seems to be the strongest. This device is for you if you are a professional craftsman who wishes to use a variety of tools, as well as if you enjoy stitching, are an avid paper craftsman, or may be a woodworker. Good FOR: Craftspeople who want it, particularly those who cut thicker items or cut a lot of cloth.

Makers' Proficiencies

Paper, hard card, and vinyl stickers are just a few of the materials that Cricut Makers can cut. If you have an upgraded model, you can even cut fabrics. It functions via an online program called Design Space. You can purchase, upload, or load your plans using this, and the device will cut them for the owners. It also has a good feature called "Print and Cut," which helps you print your template on a regular home printer and then put it into the Cricut device to be cut according to size.

You may also purchase additional cutting tools to allow your device to engrave complex designs, compose elegant calligraphy, or perforate lovely lines. As a matter of fact, the good news is that you can also use Cricut as a printer! You can load any marker (designed for this machine) into the dedicated accessory slot in your machine, and it will "draw" any template for you. Sometimes, even if your writing isn't very good, it's perfect to have a lovely handwritten feel.

Explore Air 2

With the ability to cut cardboard, suede, imitation leather, Cricut felt, and over a hundred other products, this machine is truly a powerful tool. For the majority of artisans, this is an excellent machine, but it cannot cut heavier fabrics like the manufacturer can. It also goes well in every craft room because it has a lot of colors! BEST FOR: Cutting common material like cardboard, vinyl, and iron is a common desire among consumers. (Judgement) Because you will get a lot of use out of it and it can accommodate all of the newest and greatest updates and add-ons that Cricut releases, it is the best long-term plan. These devices are undoubtedly expensive, so it's best to purchase one for yourself because it also has the power and versatility to cut with! You can cut a lot more silk, felt, wood, and leather with the help of Cricut Maker than you ever could with this set of tools—I'm in awe! Additionally, it has been beginning to offer discounts recently, so if you have an Explore series like this and are looking to update, you can get some incredible discounts on it. No matter which version you choose, you can still wirelessly connect the Cricut units to the build, create or import designs on your computer, and then turn those designs back to your Cricut device for cutting. The Cricut Design Space app, which is readily available for Windows, MAC, and Smart Phone operating systems, helps you build and import templates that can be cut with your device. A tiny blade—a scoring tool, pen, or rotary blade—is housed inside the Cricut device. When your design in Design Space is ready to cut, you can wirelessly submit it from your desktop to your Cricut device and lock your preferred material on a 12-inch wide cutting pad. You can then load the material into the machine after that. The project will begin to cut when a button is pressed.

Cricut Joy

Introducing the next machine, the little but powerful Cricut Joy. For those of us without a dedicated craft space, this machine's ability to fit a lot of features into a small, neatly-stored drawer is a tremendous bonus!

For someone who is just starting out with Cricut, this would make a fantastic Christmas present. It also happens to be the machine with the lowest price point and the most features and capabilities overall.

With a starting price of $179.99, the Joy cuts more than 50 materials. This machine can both write and cut, and it isn't print-then-cut compatible. The maximum material width is 5.5 inches, however Smart Materials allows you to purchase a 20-foot length. It also has a neat feature that lets you make cards.

What can be cut with the Cricut Joy?
Okay, so after learning that the Maker can cut more than 300 materials, 50 materials might not sound like much, but here's the problem. As a beginner or intermediate

crafter, you'll likely wish to cut through most, if not all, of the 50 materials that the Cricut Joy can cut.

Like the Explore Air 2 and the Maker, it uses a fine-point precision blade to cut a ton of complex forms. It can cut a variety of materials including vinyl, iron-on, cardstock, label paper, construction paper, cardboard, and Infusible Ink transfer sheets.

Smart Materials for Cutting Without a Mat

Cutting without a mat is a nice feature of the Cricut Joy. This was the first mat-free machine made by Cricut. If you're using Smart Materials made specifically for Cricut Joy mat, you don't need an adhesive mat.

It's okay to use ordinary materials or leftovers; all you'll need is a tiny Cricut Joy mat. It cuts as much as 20 feet long without a mat, but its greatest breadth is significantly smaller—5.5 inches. I adore this feature. It can create a single image up to 4 feet long.

The Joy is a machine that can write like other machines. You cannot use Explore Air 2/Maker pens on Joy due to size difference. For the small Joy, everything is sized down. However, the Joy's writing feature is very fantastic, especially since it allows you to use pre-made label paper!

The Cricut Joy mat also includes a design that is intended exclusively for cardmaking, which is another wonderful feature. A design is cut into a card stock sleeve for the card cutting to function. The design really pops when you place a card inside the sleeve that is a different color.

Cricut Joy Xtra

This is an improved model of the Cricut Joy. It is just as capable as the Joy, but it can cut shapes up to 8.5 inches wide due to its greater cutting size. Additionally, print-then-cut is supported on the Joy Xtra.

It can cut more than 50 materials, just as the Joy, and has a base price of $199. Everything that you most likely wish to cut. It foils, writes, and draws.

What can be cut with the Joy Xtra?

Everything that the Joy can cut, including vinyl, iron-on, cardboard, paper, labels, and more, may also be cut with the Joy Xtra. When using a mat, the Joy Xtra can cut to an A4 letter size, or 8.5 by 11 inches.

Additionally, the Joy Xtra is compatible with Smart Materials. With Joy Xtra Smart Materials, you may cut up to 4 feet long and 8.5 inches wide. Of course, a mat is not necessary while using the Smart Materials.

It is possible to use the Smart Materials on both a Joy and a Joy Xtra. However, you have a larger cut range if you go with the Joy Xtra. This implies that you can cut multiple smaller or larger designs at once.

The Joy Xtra is also praised for its print-then-cut feature as well. You know what it means? Stickers! Stickers are something you can make! Of course, printable vinyl and iron-on can also be created using the print-then-cut feature. This means that the Joy Xtra has a ton of features that the regular Joy does not. This machine is excellent for both novice and seasoned makers.

Cricut Venture

Cricut Venture is Cricut's attempt at large-format cutting. Cricut promises to create elegant, user-friendly machines, and this one delivers both amazing precision and commercial speed.

The Venture does not lie flat, which is something you will notice right away. This means that you do not load it from the front. Rather, the larger machine is positioned at a 45-degree angle. By eliminating the requirement for space in front of and behind the machine when using mats, that contributes to space conservation.

The Venture can cut over 100 various types of materials, including vinyl, iron-on, paper, leather, poster board, and bonded fabric. Its base price is $999.

The Venture's size and cutting speed are its two primary selling factors. Let's discuss the two. The Venture cuts quickly—up to 25 inches per second. The Venture is a fantastic option if you are a small business owner looking to cut a large number of the same design swiftly.

The Cricut Venture is capable of cutting materials up to 24 inches wide when using Smart Materials. which is twice the width of regular Cricut machines. It can cut repeated/separate images up to 75 feet long and single images up to 12 feet long.

This machine can also be used to cut using a mat. Made of a more durable material, the Venture mats are performance machine mats. It is important to note that other Cricut machine mates are not compatible with the Venture and will break and distort when the pinch rollers apply pressure.

Which Cricut machine should you buy?

Now that we've considered all the major types of Cricut machines, I know you might be wondering which to buy?; that question can only be answered after considering this fact list below. Below is a list that points out the selling point of each of the Cricut machines and why they might be ideal for you;

- *Cricut Explore Air 2*: Ideal for makers on a tight budget, this versatile and reasonably priced alternative is great for novices who wish to work with various materials but don't need the most advanced features.
- *Cricut Explore Air 3*: If you desire the features of the Explore Air 2 plus the added convenience of cutting without a mat while using Smart Materials, the Cricut Explore Air 3 is a good option. It has faster cutting speeds and smoother performance when compared to the Explore Air 2.
- *Cricut Maker*: Designed for dedicated craftsmen who require accuracy and adaptability, This device is capable of cutting a variety of materials including leather and wood, making it a versatile tool for all your cutting needs.
- *Cricut Maker 3*: This model is comparable to the first Maker but has the added benefit of being able to cut without a mat when using Smart Materials. It is the perfect option for users who need quick tool changes and desire the benefits of longer, faster cuts.
- *The Cricut Joy*: The Cricut Joy is the most economical machine and the perfect choice for small-scale projects. It is also compact and affordable.
- *Cricut Joy Xtra:* This versatile and reasonably priced option suits novice and seasoned crafters. It has all the features of the Joy but with a bigger cutting size; in contrast, it can print before cutting and utilizes mat-less Smart Materials.
- *The Cricut Venture*: Suitable for small company owners or users who need to cut large amounts rapidly, the Cricut Venture is built for large-format cutting and commercial speed. It is perfect for creating large-scale projects and is compatible with Smart Materials.

BOOK 2:
UNBOXING YOUR CRICUT

You've chosen the right Cricut cut for you, then. You either picked it up at the craft store or carefully waited for it to come in the mail. Today is the big day! It's time to take your brand-new Cricut out of the box! Are you happy? I believe Cricut owners can be put into two groups:

1. Those who open their Cricut box right away.
2. Those who, despite wanting to start creating more than any other thing, leave their Cricut in the box for months.

No matter what group you're in, It's really simple to take your Cricut out of the box and set it up for the first time. To help you get your Cricut out of the box and start having fun with it, I'll walk you through each step.

You have the option of buying either the machine itself or a machine bundle when you buy your Cricut Maker or Cricut Explore Air 2 from the Cricut website. A lot of craft shops only sell the machine itself, not groups of them. You will get a machine whether you buy one or not.

Your Cricut kit will arrive in a box, and each box will contain the same fundamental components. These are them:

- Your Cricut Cutting Machine
- Cutting Mat
- Power Cord
- USB Cord For Connecting Your Cricut To Your Computer
- A Pen
- Cutting Blade
- Packet called "Let's Get Started"

There will be a manual, a step-by-step guide on how to set up your new machine, materials for a new project, and a Cricut Access trial membership in this.

Let's start taking your machine out of the box!

- Take everything out of the box and make sure all the parts are there for your machine. The list of parts that come with your machine is on the side of the box.
- Move the plastic cover off your Cricut machine
- Now open the "Let's Get Started" package.
- Plug in the power line and turn your Cricut over.
- Follow the steps at cricut.com/setup to connect your Cricut when you're on Windows, Mac, IOS, or Android.

Note: If you already have a Cricut, you can go straight to Design Space by going to cricut.com/setup. Your Cricut will connect to your computer when you plug in the USB cord. Once you choose a project to make, click "Make It," and Design Space will connect to your new machine.

Go to https://tinyurl.com/cricutbluetooth to learn how to use Bluetooth to connect your Cricut to Windows, Mac, IOS, or Android.

Step 6: It's time to make! The project that comes with your Cricut is great for people who have never used one before! As one of your first projects, we think you should make some bling for your Cricut! It is simple. Go to page 51 of the book to see our #Creative Cricut Bling art project. This is a simple project that you can do on your first Cricut project. You can make something that you'll see every time you use your Cricut, which will help you remember it!

Essential Cricut Materials for Beginners

Vinyl Adhesive vinyl is the first material I would suggest buying and a must-have for Cricut users. It is ideal for customizing products like mugs, phone covers, and home decor because it is available in various hues, textures, and designs. Stick with the Cricut brand when looking for sticky vinyl because it is designed to fit your Cricut machine flawlessly. After experimenting with other manufacturers, I've found that Cricut's vinyl works best for weeding (removing extra vinyl from surrounding my design) and applying.

Since Smart Vinyl works with the Maker 3 and Explore Machines, Weeding this stuff cutting doesn't require a Machine Mat. It is ideal for continuous or exceptionally lengthy cuts up to 12 feet long and is available in both permanent and detachable versions.

The best vinyl to use with a Cricut Maker or Cricut Explore Air 2 is premium vinyl. Moreover, based on the project you want to construct, it is available in both permanent and removable options. To cut it, a machine mat is needed.

Iron-On HTV (Heat Transfer Vinyl)

Heat transfer vinyl, sometimes referred to as iron-on or HTV, is the best option if you want to personalize clothes, purses, or other fabric products. For a durable and polished surface, make sure you adhere to Cricut's cutting, weeding, and HTV application directions. For the longest-lasting finish, I suggest applying your iron-on to your item with a Cricut EasyPress.

Similar to Smart Vinyl, Smart Iron-On may be cut without a machine mat. This material is a dream to work with, and the Cricut Maker 3 or Explore 3 cuts it incredibly fast, which is why I adore it. For extra-length designs, it is also available in rolls up to 12 feet long.

Daily Iron-On is an additional excellent option. It comes in various colors and requires a machine mat for cutting. Oftentimes, Cricut offers good discounts on bulk variety pack iron-ons, such as this multicolored one.

Cardstock

A excellent medium for crafting paper goods including scrapbook pages, greeting cards, and home décor is cardboard. Select a premium material that works with your Cricut machine (65 lb. or heavier is typical). Try with various hues, patterns, and coatings to give your creations more variation.

The Cardstock Samplers from Cricut are an excellent place to start. This cardstock has a wonderful texture, and at 80 pounds, it's nice and thick for a range of crafts, including card crafting and scrapbooking.

Key Items to Include in Your Cricut Toolbox

A Design Space with a Cricut and Desktop Computer: You will need a computer and Cricut Design Space software in order to operate your machine. Although you can use the Design Space app on your phone or tablet, a desktop or laptop computer with access to Design Space is what I suggest in order to get the most out of the application. I create my Cricut designs using Design Space on both my computer and my phone.

Blades: A premium fine point blade is included with your Cricut machine, but for cutting thicker materials like chipboard and heavy cardstock, you might also wish to get a deep point blade (compatible with Cricut Maker & Explore machines).

Another blade/tool is the Rotary Blade. Though it works exclusively with the Maker, this is an excellent tool for cutting crepe paper and fabric.

Basic Tool Set for Lifting & Weeding: Using weeding tools makes it simpler to transfer designs onto the surface of your product by removing extra material from your cuts. The standard weeding tool kit need to comprise of a scraper, scissors, tweezers, and a hook. Another necessity is a spatula, which is ideal for gently removing delicate cutouts from your cutting mat without causing any damage. Because it includes every necessary tool you would need to weed and transfer your patterns, I appreciate the Cricut Basic Tool Set. Additionally, there is the Basic Tool Set, which includes a trimmer and scoring stylus among other equipment.

If you want to work with cardstock for crafts like paper flowers and greeting cards, you might wish to include a scoring stylus in your tool box. It produces lovely scoring lines for folding.

Transfer Tape: Adhesive vinyl designs must be moved from their backside to the project surface using transfer tape. The grid-lined transfer tape from Cricut comes in two grip sizes: standard and strong, making alignment simple. Most vinyl can be used with Regular Transfer Tape, while Strong Grip Transfer Tape is necessary for thicker vinyl, such as glitter vinyl.

Cricut EasyPress

Cricut EasyPress is a necessary tool for creating a more polished & durable result. The EasyPress has a built-in timer that you can set in addition to adjusting the temperature so you can precisely time how long to press your design for optimal results. EasyPress is ideal for most of my projects, including labels, tote bags, and t-shirts.

Extra Cricut Accessories, Materials, and Tools

Apart from the aforementioned essential Cricut items for novices, the following add-ons might enhance your Cricut creative endeavors.

Cricut Access Subscription: Although you may upload your own photos and use some free fonts in Cricut Design Space, I strongly advise getting a Cricut Access Subscription. If you frequently use your Cricut and would like access to over 300,000 images and thousands of ready-to-make projects, this is really helpful.

Brayer: For a smoother cut and improved adherence, use a brayer, which is a little roller, to press materials onto your cutting mat.

XL Scraper: For larger projects, an XL scraper is useful since it makes applying transfer tape and smoothing out bubbles easier.

Although a Standard Grip mat is included with your Cricut machine, you may find that LightGrip or StrongGrip Cricut mats are more helpful when working with thinner or heavier materials, respectively. If you wish to utilize Smart Materials alone and you have the Cricut Explore 3 or Maker 3, you won't have to bother about using any mats at all.

Trimmer: You can cut vinyl and paper materials precisely straight with the aid of a portable trimmer. If you work with longer rolls of Smart Materials, the integrated trimmer on the Cricut Roll Holder is a great addition to the tool.

Infusible Ink: If you want to give your work a very polished appearance, playing with ink might be entertaining. Smooth and polished, the ink melts straight into the cloth (or mug, if you're using the Cricut Mug Press).

BOOK 3:
THE CRICUT DESIGN SPACE

When you set up your Cricut machine, the company will instantly ask you to download Design Space. Click on the Cricut C application icon to open the program once you've got it. Cricut Design Space also has an app that people who use iOS and Android can get. You might just have to look around to find where each tool is because the features between the PC top version and the app version of Design Space are all very similar.

First Look

A home screen with a lot of choices for things you can do will appear when you open Cricut Design Space. There are photos of Cricut machines and supplies you can buy from the site along the top of the screen that you can click on. You may also see an ad for Cricut Access. We'll talk more about that later.

You'll see a section called "My Projects" below the ads. It has a box with a plus sign inside a circle that says "New Project."

After that, you'll see a list of different types of ready-to-make projects. These are projects that Cricut, Cricut brand partners, and Cricut Community Members have already designed. All you have to do is press a button to cut them out.

A green A can be seen in some of the photos. If you have a Cricut Access account, this cut file is free for you to use, as indicated by the green A, which is a symbol for Cricut Access.

Cricut Access is a paid service that gives you quick, free access to more than 100,000 images, 100+ fonts, and hundreds of ready-to-make projects. Members of Cricut Access also get a deal when they buy things from Cricut, like supplies from Cricut.com and licensed images through Design Space.

You will have the opportunity to test out the cutting service Cricut Access when you buy a Cricut cutting machine because it comes with a free trial membership good for one month.

The images, fonts, and ready-to-make projects can be used by anyone, regardless of whether or not they have a Cricut Access membership. You will only be required to pay a nominal fee for the very first time that you make use of them.

Setting Up a blank Background

You'll be taken to a blank Cricut canvas when you click on the "New Project" button. There are three lines stacked on top of each other in the upper left corner of the screen.

Before you cut your projects, the Cricut Machine and Design Space Canvas are the place where the entirety of the magic happens. Configuration Space is the place where you clean and sort your manifestations. You can utilize Cricut's superior text and visual styles through individual purchases, Cricut Access, and Cartridges in this space in addition to being able to transfer and use your own text styles and pictures.

Since you will constantly require this product to cut any length, investing in a Cricut is useless if you can't master Design Space. In spite of the fact that Cricut Design Space looks complicated, it is a fantastic instrument for beginners. If you haven't used other design programs such as Photoshop or Illustrator, don't worry, using this program is very simple. If you have experience using any Adobe Creative Cloud applications or Inkscape, you'll quickly find this program intuitive and easy to use. However, even if you're new to design programs like Photoshop or Illustrator, you'll find that it's straightforward to get started. On the other hand, if you're familiar with Adobe Creative Cloud apps or Inkscape, you'll find this program a breeze to use. I hope this helps. However, if you have used any of Adobe's Creative Cloud apps or Inkscape before, you will find this one to be a breeze. I really do hope this is useful. If you're unfamiliar with graphic design software like Adobe Photoshop or Illustrator, you'll find that learning this one is a breeze. That being said, if you know use Adobe Creative Cloud apps or Inkscape, you will find this program very easy to use. Small structures and tasks can be created with the help of Shapes and Fonts in Configuration Space. If you want to make something more complex, you'll need access to your own Cricut Access or Cricut Cut. Through that door, you can get into their huge library. Every time you log in to Cricut Design Space and need to begin or alter a task, you will do so from a window called Canvas. The Canvas Area in Cricut Design Space is where you complete the entirety of your editing before you cut your projects.

There are so many buttons, choices, and activities that you might get tired of them. Try not to stress about this subject while traveling; instead, cut things up to wake you up and encourage you to keep going. With this subject, you will realize what EVERY ICON on the Canvas area is used for. We're going to divide the canvas into four areas and four colors to keep everything under control and straightforward. The top panel is yellow and is the editing area. The left panel is blue and is the insert area. The right panel is purple and is the layers panel. The last panel is green and is the canvas area.

Let's talk about each of these panels one by one.

Top Panel

Components on the canvas zone can be altered and arranged using the top panel of the Design Space Canvas. From this panel, you can pick which sort of text style you prefer to utilize, as well as change sizes and designs. However, this design is not just limited to these options. This panel is further broken down into two smaller pieces. The first enables you to spare, name, and then cut your ventures. In addition, the next one will let you alter and control things on the canvas area. We should look into each of these screens separately. The main panel enables you to move from the Canvas to your task, profile, and it also sends your finished projects to cut.

Toggle Menu

The first part here is Toggle Menu. This option will open a whole new menu when you click on it. A convenient menu is provided. But it's not part of the Canvas, which is why I won't go into a ton of detail. Basically, this is where you can change your picture and go to your profile. You can also change your machine or sharp edges, as well as update the Firmware, or Software, of your gadget, from this Menu. These are additional helpful and specialized things you can do. The memberships you get from Cricut Access, managing your account, and a lot more can all be done from this menu. The best thing to do is to click on each button so that you can see what Cricut Design Space has designed for you. Additionally, you can change your account's settings and Canvas' estimations.

All undertakings and projects initiate with a "Untitled" title, you can give a name to a task from the canvas region after you've set in one component.

My Project

Whenever you choose to click my projects, you will then, be diverted to your library of things you have just made. This is extraordinary in light of the fact that occasionally you may need to re-cut a recently made undertaking. In this way, there's no requirement for you to reproduce a similar task again and again. Then comes the choice Save, which will enact after you've put one component on your canvas region. I suggest you save your projects as you go along the task. In spite of the fact that the product is on the cloud, if your program crashes, there goes your difficult work with it.

Make

When you are finished transferring your records and prepared to cut, just click on Make it. Your activities are partitioned by mats as indicated by the shades of your task. From this window, you can likewise expand the number of tasks to cut. This is incredible in the event that you are anticipating making more than one cut.

Editing panel

It will assist you with editing, mastermind, and compose text styles and pictures on the Canvas Area. It incorporates Undo and Redo. Now and then, while we work, we may make mistakes. These little buttons are an incredible method to address them. Snap Undo when you make something you don't care for, or make a mix-up. Snap Redo when you unintentionally erase something you would not like to erase or change.

Line type and Fill

This alternative will mention to your machine what devices and cutting edges you are going to utilize. Remember that relying upon the Machine you have chosen on the highest point of the window, you will have various choices. The next one is the Cut choice. Except if you transferred a JPEG or PNG picture to the Canvas. The cut is the default line type that the entirety of your components on your canvas will have. This implies when you press Make It, your machine will cut those designs. With the Cut alternative chose, you can change the fill of your components, toward the day's end, this interprets in the various shades of materials you will utilize when you cut your activities. When you select a specific design, the design on your canvas area will be sketched out with the pen you selected.

Engrave, Deboss, Wave, and Perf.

These are the most recent devices that Cricut has released for the Cricut Maker machine, and with them, you will have the ability to make as printing results for various kinds of materials defining different design.

Select All

The next option is Select All, which will enable you to cut, copy, and paste components from the canvas.

Align Left will veer off the center of the content to one side. Center Horizontal will actuate the center of the content to one side.

Distribute horizontally will alter the components horizontally. The farthest left and right design will determine the length of the dispersion. Distribute vertically will alter the components vertically.

Arrange

When you work with various components, options, and designs, the new component you add to the canvas will always be in front of every other component.

Size

All that you make or type in Cricut Design Space has a size. You can change the size from the component in self. In any case, if you need a thing to have a definite estimation, this choice will enable you to do as such. Something basic is the little lock. When you increment or diminish the size of a picture, the extents are constantly bolted. By tapping on the little lock, you are telling the program that you would prefer not to keep similar measurements. Alike to size, rotating a component is something you can do rapidly from the canvas area. Be that as it may, a few designs should be turned on a particular edge. If that is the situation for you, I prescribe you to utilize this capacity. Else, you will invest so a lot of energy battling to get a component calculated the manner in which you need it to be. The position box gives you where your things are on the canvas area when you click on a particular design. You can move your components around by indicating where you need that component to be situated on the canvas areas.

Flip Horizontal will cut your text or design horizontally. It's convenient when you're attempting to make a left and right design.

With the Capacity Space, this content native will handle the space between letters in a passage; this would be precarious in light of the fact that occasionally I am compelled to move a single line of text.

The Left Panel

The left panel is adorned with embedding shapes, pictures, projects, and other things that are ready to be cut.

New

which enables you to insert and replace another project in the canvas area. The second one is Templates, which enables you to look at various layouts of the projects you are going to create.

Except if you have Cricut Access, there are a few important things you need to think about on this board: Cricut Images, prepared to cut tasks, and Cricut text control styles cost money. If you use them, you must pay before you cut your task. Let's see what you get by clicking on these panels.

The first is when you click on NEW, and if you are currently working on a project, you will see a warning over the canvas asking you whether you want to replace your project or not. If you need to replace your project, make a spare window to save all of the changes from the current canvas; otherwise, you will lose your completed project.

If you need to customize style instruments, this one is brilliant on the grounds that you can choose sizes and various types of attire. Additionally, they have a ton of different classes that you can look over. Keep in mind that templates are only for you to envision and perceive how your instrument will fit in a pre-defined size.

You can also choose Projects, which is where you should go if you want to start cutting right away. Once you choose your task, you can redo it or have Snap-On make it, and then follow the cutting instructions. Most of the projects are free for Cricut Access members, or you can buy them as you go. If you want to see which ones are free, just look at the bottom of the categories drop-down menu and select "Free."

Images

Images are great for putting together your own projects; they give your artworks an extra touch and personality. You can search by keywords, categories, or cartridges. Cartridges are groups of pictures that you have to buy separately. Some of them come with Cricut Access, like Disney, Sesame Street, Hello Kitty, and so on. Cricut has free pictures to cut and color.

Text

When you need to type on the Canvas Area, tap on Text; a small window that says Add text here will open on the canvas.

Shapes

Having the option to use shapes is pretty useful and basic. They let you make simple, excellent projects that aren't too complicated. You can choose from nine shapes: Square, Triangle, Pentagon, Hexagon, Star, Octagon, and Heart.

Upload

 This is where you can upload your files and pictures. The internet is full of them; a lot of bloggers make projects for free.

The Right Panel (layers)

Layers refer to all the parts or structures on the canvas area. Think of it like clothing: your outfit has different layers, which can be simple or complicated depending on the day or season. For example, on a cold day, your layers would include pants, a shirt, a coat, socks, boots, gloves, and so on. On a hot day, you would only need one layer, which would be your swimsuit.

Maybe a message that says "Merry Christmas," a tree, the card itself, and maybe even an envelope? My point is that all of those little plans and parts are layers. Some layers can be changed, but others, like JPEG and PNG images, can't because of how the file or layer is designed.

Group, Ungroup, Duplicate, and Delete

These settings—Group, Ungroup, Duplicate, and Delete—will help you move things around the canvas more easily, so play around with them.

Group

Click this to group all the layers. This setting is useful when you have a lot of layers that make up a complicated plan.

Suppose you are working on an elephant. The elephant will definitely be made up of different layers, like the body, eyes, legs, abdomen, and so on. If you want to add more shapes and content, you will probably be moving the elephant around the canvas a lot. By grouping all of the elephant layers together, you can make sure that everything stays in place when you move them around the canvas.

Ungroup

If you select any grouped layers on the canvas area or layers board, this option will ungroup them. Use this option if you need to change the size, type of text style, etc. of a particular part or layer from the group.

"Duplicate."

This will make a copy of any layers or plans you've chosen on the layers board or canvas.

Delete

This choice will get rid of any parts you've picked out on the canvas or layers board.

Anything on the Layers Panel will show you what Line type or Fill you are using, such as Cut, Write, Score, Perf, Wavy, Print, and so on.

Layer Visibility

The little eye on each layer on the layers board shows how visible a plan is. If you're not sure if a part looks good, you can click on the little eye to hide it instead of erasing it. Note: When you hide something, the eye will have a cross inside it. You can move a plan on top or below by tapping on a layer and dragging it; you could say this works like the Arrang tool.

Blank Canvas

This "layer" enables you to change the canvas of your canvas; in the event that you are attempting to perceive how a specific structure looks with an alternative shading. The intensity of this shading is released when you use it in conjunction with the Templates layer because you can change the shading and the layer of the layout itself.

These tools—Slice, Weld, Attach, Flatten, and Contour—are incredibly important, so make sure you know how to use them perfectly. There's no need to go into more detail because they each deserve their own lessons.

Slice

The slice tool is great for cutting out shapes, content, and other parts from different plans. When you chose the two shapes and tapped on slice, you could see that the first record got all cut up. To see what the final result was, reorder the "slice result" and then pick out all the pieces that were cut out.

Weld

which enables you to combine at least two shapes into one. When you chose the two shapes and tapped on Weld, you could see that it made a completely new shape. The shading is determined by the layer that is on the back, which is the reason the new shape is pink in shading.

Attach

Attach performs the same function as grouping layers, but with significantly more power. When you chose the two shapes and pressed "attach," you could see that the layers only changed color to match the layer that was on the back of the document.

Flatten

This tool helps with the Print, Cut, and Fill settings. If you change the fill scenario to "no fill to print," that may only affect one layer. Set up a scene where you can do it to multiple cuts at once. When you're done with your design, select all the layers you want to print, and then click on Flatten. When you're done with your design (you can't change this in the wa file),

Contour

The Contour tool lets you hide parts of a plan that you don't want to show, and it can be used when a shape or configuration has parts that you don't want to show. For this example, use the weld tool to make the first plan fit like a fiddle. Then, type in "contour" and cut it out of the new shape. Finally, use the Contour tool to hide the inside circles of the two O's and the inside part of the letter R.

Color Sync

Your canvas area is comprised of a variety of colors, each of which corresponds to a distinct color of material. Are you certain that you need all of the different shades of blue or yellow that you've used in your design? Click and drag the tone you want to remove and drop it on the one you want to keep if you only need one shade of yellow, like this model. This model can be used if you only need one yellow shade.

Canvas Area

The canvas area is where you see all of your structures and parts. It's natural and easy to use! The first one in Canvas Area is Canvas Grid and Measurements. The canvas area is separated by a framework. This is great because every square you see on the Grid makes you think of the cutting mat. Finally, this will help you make the most of your space.

Selection

 If you select at least one layer, the selection will be blue, and you can change it from all four corners. The "red x" deletes layers. The right upper corner rotates the picture (though if you need a specific point, I suggest using the turning tool on the editing menu). The lower right button, "the little lock," keeps the size re-sized.

Last but not least, you can find on a bigger or smaller scale (without changing the actual size of your plans) by pressing the "+" and "-" buttons in the bottom left area of the canvas. That's all there is to this Cricut Design Space.

Cricut smart set dial: Once you've made your project and are ready to cut, score, or write, you should set the Smart Set Dial to the type of material you have on your tangle. The dial has simple settings for paper, vinyl, iron-on, light cardstock, cardstock with reinforced texture, and notice board. This makes it easy to figure out what settings you need for cut weight, number of cuts, and type of sharp edge.

To cut, line up your material straight on your cutting mat. In this case, I need to cut out cardstock flowers for my cards. Find the tangle in the machine and click on the glimmering bolt button. This will stack the tangle in the machine ready to cut. Make sure your Smart Set Dial is set to the cardstock setting and press the C button. This will tell the machine to cut out your shape.

BOOK 4:
CRICUT PROJECTS

If you already own a Cricut, what should you make with it? With a Cricut, you can create nearly anything, which can be too much if you don't know what to make or have recently purchased the machine. To inspire you, we've compiled a list of 30 entertaining and original Cricut project ideas.

Things to know

- Some of these projects require the Cricut Cut Maker 3, but the majority may be finished with any Cricut.

- Some projects could need accessories from Cricut, like the mug press or heat press.

- If you wish to sell things that you made with your Cricut, you must not include designs, figures, or other intellectual property rights protected assets.

Matching T-Shirts

Purchase matching shirts for your family or party. Certain activities, such as family vacations, holiday photos, or being a part of a club or Greek life at school, may require you to wear matching shirts. Any statement, picture, or name you desire can be used to make a one-of-a-kind t-shirt design with a Cricut. Because you can print the same design several times, you can also quickly make a lot of shirts.

It is possible to carry out this plan effectively with nothing more than a Cricut machine, some heat transfer vinyl (HTV), or sheets of infusible ink. When it comes to transferring your design, you can achieve the same results with an iron as you would with a Cricut cut heat press. You just need to set your iron to the appropriate temperature.

Wearables With A Brand Name

Make items such as hoodies, shirts, and other things with your own logo. If you run a business, custom-branded products are a terrific way to advertise your company and make extra money. But having these things made by someone else might be expensive, particularly if you only sell them as a trial. With a Cricut, you can make as many branded products as you like, meaning you'll never have too many that you can't sell.

To make this plan, you can use any Cricut machine and heat-transfer vinyl (HTV) or infusible ink sheets. An iron will work just as well as a Cricut cut heat press to transfer your design.

Art Shirts

Print your work on a t-shirt to display it to the world. If you are an artist, you can use your work to make one-of-a-kind graphic t-shirts that show off your style and art. A high-resolution digital art work might be used to make a large print shirt, or you could place a smaller piece where a pocket would be, on the sleeve or across the chest.

This design can be made with any Cricut machine and heat-transfer vinyl (HTV) or sheets of infusible ink. Infusible ink may work better for this project if you are making a large transfer. Any iron will do, but the Cricut heat press makes the process of transferring your design very simple.

Custom Pillow Case Design

Make pillowcases that match the color scheme or furniture in your room. Finding the right pillow case can be challenging if your sheet set didn't include one. However, if you own a Cricut, you may make your own pillow cases that fit (or contrast with) the rest of the decor in your room. Consider buying plain pillowcases in a color other than your bedding and using your Cricut to cut a similar design.

To make this project, you can use any Cricut machine and heat-transfer vinyl (HTV) or infusible ink sheets. Any iron will do, but the Cricut heat press makes the process of transferring your design very simple.

Business Mugs

Custom-made mugs can be made for your employees or to sell.

Custom-made mugs can be made for your employees or to sell. In addition to making branded wearables, making branded cups is a fantastic way to market your business and make terrific gifts to give to your staff. Because you can safely make several copies of the same thing using your Cricut tip, the mugs will appear just as nice as ones made by a professional.

Any Cricut machine and infusible ink sheets can be used to create this idea, but you will need a Cricut mug press.

Gift-Sized Customized Mugs

People you care about who enjoy tea or coffee should receive gifts. Making them personalized mugs is a terrific gift if you have relatives or friends that use them a lot. Consider their favorite book passage, photos of enjoyable experiences you've had together, their favorite animal, or a catchphrase or slogan when coming up with design ideas.

Any Cricut machine and infusible ink sheets can be used to create this idea, but you will need a Cricut mug press.

Personalized Mugs

Create mugs with your own custom name on them. An excellent approach to showcase a unique monogram design is with a personalized mug. Products with monograms are stylish and well-liked. If you don't have a drawn monogram, you can make one with typography by using various font sizes to create a cohesive design.

Any Cricut machine and infusible ink sheets can be used to create this idea, but you will need a Cricut mug press.

BOOK 5:
VINYL CRICUT DESIGNS

This section is going to be about vinyl. With vinyl, it's too much pleasure. If, as a child, you like stickers, you would adore cutting vinyl with your Cricut. It's similar to making stickers of your own choosing, which you can wear with practically everything! As with vinyl patterns,

Vinyl is available in a dizzying array of colors, surface textures, and patterning options. Holographic, matte, glossy, chalkboard, dry erase, and even glow-in-the-dark variations are all available for this product.

When buying vinyl for a project, the number one question you need to think about is how long you want it to last.

Vinyl can be broken down into four main groups:

Put this on anything that will get wet that needs to be waterproof.

Whether that means being washed with your dishes or left out in the weather. Note: You can also get permanent outdoor vinyl, which is best for projects that will be in the sun, rain, or snow. This vinyl is great for shower doors, glasses, mugs, and more.

Removable vinyl: Removable vinyl can be moved without leaving any traces up to two years after it was applied. When you don't need to wash something, you can use vinyl that can be taken off. Removable vinyl is still effective, but you can peel it off if you need to for some other reason. It's great for making home signs, wall stickers, notebook covers, mirror quotes, Cricut decorations, and more.

Permanent vinyl: Use permanent vinyl on everything that can get wet, whether it's being cleaned outside or indoors, such as your dishes. (Note: sturdy outdoor vinyl is also available and is typically a superior choice for projects exposed to heat, rain, and snow.) Perfect for shower doors, mugs, glasses, and more.

Printable vinyl: Print designs using your home printer and the Cricut's print and cut feature. It's great for making planner stickers, party decorations, quick and easy projects, and more.

Applying heat to heat transfer vinyl (also called HTV or iron-on) will make it stick to fabric, paper, wood, and other surfaces for good.

To begin cutting vinyl with a Cricut, you will need the following supplies:

Supplies

- The Cricut Machine
- Vinyl
- Basic tool set for Cricut

Directions

Create a new project or launch your existing one: To begin, launch Cricut Design Space and either create a new project or open one that has been saved. You can load your own project or use images from the Cricut library. You can also make a Make It Now image.

Get your project ready for cutting: You may definitely skip these next few steps if you're working on a Make It Now project or utilizing an image from the Cricut image library; those images are typically all ready to go directly to the machine with no additional work required!

Here are some easy tips for handling groups, colors, and layers if you've uploaded your own image (a jpeg or svg file) so it's ready for cutting.

By clicking the green Make It button that is found in the top right corner of the screen, you will be able to determine whether or not your image is prepared to be trimmed.

- The Cricut is ready to cut a three-layered image file out of vinyl.

- You're set to go if the subsequent screen shows your image properly spaced and aligned, divided into mats by layers or colors.

- Proceed to Send Your Image To The Machine For Cutting after skipping the remainder of this stage. For instance, the image below shows three distinct mats, one for each color of the heart, and the shapes are all evenly spaced.

How to use a Cricut machine to cut vinyl in multiple colors

- If the screen that appears after "smushed", with the shapes color-separated but not properly spaced, you should click the grey Cancel button to go back and make some changes before sending the design to your Cricut for cutting.

- Using a Cricut, cut the detachable image file out of vinyl.

- The shapes in Cricut Design Space must be "Attached" in order to maintain proper image spacing.

- Alternatively, you might click on each red-striped layer in the Layers window on the right by holding down Shift.

- Using a Cricut machine, attach all shapes of the same color to cut vinyl in various colors.

- When you have finished selecting everything that is a single color, click the Attach icon, which looks like a square made of grey and is located in the lower right corner of the Layers panel.
- When the layers are attached, any changes you make to the size or position of the image will result in the layers moving together as a unit.

- Instead of seeing the layers as a collection of separate shapes that can be rotated or cut to fit, it will compel them to align precisely as they show on the screen when cutting.

- Continue with any additional "group" of shapes that require appropriate spacing.

- Provide your image to the cutting machine,

- After attaching each of your various colors, send the image to your machine for cutting by clicking the green Make It button.

- Based only on color, your design will be automatically divided into multiple mats. This allows you to cut out multiple colored or layered designs in a single project!

- To make several copies of your project, edit the Project Copies box. If you're cutting iron-on vinyl, make sure to turn on the Mirror switch after you've set the Material Size for each mat. On the mat preview to the right, you can also move the images as you see fit. (If you are creating several copies, this will help you line up the images.)

- Click the green Continue button when everything appears to be in order.

- You can essentially just follow the on-screen directions from this point on! Verify that the Connect Machine window at the top of the screen shows your Cricut machine is turned on. Adjust the machine's Smart Dial to Vinyl; alternatively, use Cricut's vinyl cut settings guidance if your machine is older and lacks a smart dial.

- To cut vinyl, load the first cutting mat into the Cricut machine.

- Ensure that the vinyl is adhered to the cutting mat with the paper backing facing downward.

- Place adhesive vinyl over a Cricut cutting mat

- Proceed to insert the mat into your Cricut machine by pressing the Load/Unload button, which will flash.

- To cut vinyl, load the cutting mat into the Cricut machine.

- The screen will instruct you to press the blinking Go button after the mat has been loaded.

- Use a Cricut machine to cut vinyl into multiple layers or colors.

- As your machine completes the cut, the screen will show a progress meter. The screen will indicate that you need to unload your cutting mat by pressing the Load/Unload button once it has finished cutting.

- To cut vinyl in various colors, load a second vinyl color into the Cricut machine.

- If you have a second or third color of vinyl to cut, carefully peel the previous color of vinyl off the cutting mat, and then place the new color of vinyl on top of the cut. After the Load/Unload button has started flashing, the cutting mat can be loaded into the machine by pressing the button. After that, you need to hit the Go button. Carry on cutting mats up until they are all finished.

- When you're satisfied with the final product, click the green Finish button to return to your work. Place the cutting mat down.

- The background vinyl can now be removed and used for your project! Use transfer paper if you have several pieces and want to ensure that the vinyl is transferred to your project with the proper spacing.

- Peel the transfer paper backing and press it on top of the weeded-out vinyl to keep the design. Press hard for adhesion.

- Then, peel up the transfer paper. Once the vinyl is positioned and firmly pressed onto your project, carefully peel away the transfer tape to reveal the vinyl.

There are other terms and vinyl related items that you might need to know, these include the following:

Weeding: Weeding is the process of getting rid of the empty space around your design. So, for example, if you have your Cricut cut a "O," you would need to move the extra vinyl from around the outside of your O and the inside of your O, leaving only the letter on the back of the paper.

Print and Cut: Print and Cut is a tool in Cricut Design Space that allows you to print out a design using your home printer and then have your Cricut cut it out for you.

Oracal 631: Oracal 631 is a brand of waterproof vinyl that a lot of skilled crafters use. Finish in matte. Ideal for wall stickers, stencils, and other designs you might want to move later.

Oracal 651: Oracal 651 is a brand of permanent vinyl that artists use a lot. Glossy finish, safe to use outside. Ideal for signs, stickers, and mugs that will stay on.

Burnishing: Burnishing is the process of using a scraper or brayer tool to rub transfer tape that has been placed over the top of the vinyl to help it stick to the surface.

Kiss Cut: The kiss cut only cuts through the top layer of a material. Vinyl and HTV both use a kiss cut. In this case, your machine will only cut the vinyl and not the back paper. This is something that your Cricut will do for you if you set it to the right material.

Fine-tip cutting blade: This is the best blade for cutting vinyl and most other common materials, like iron-on, cardboard, scrapbook paper, and more.

Regular grip cutting mat: This type of cutting mat has the right grip to keep your vinyl in place while you cut it, and then you can remove it without messing up the design.

Transfer tape: The transfer tape comes in two different grips: normal grip, which works for most vinyl, and StrongGrip, which works best for "specialty" vinyl like shimmer and glitter. Transfer tape moves vinyl from its paper backing to its desired location. Clear transfer tape with a grid pattern helps me place and align my design.

Weeding tools are especially helpful when weeding small letters and intricate designs because they help you move the extra vinyl. With HTV, cleaning tools are also utilized.

Cricut Bright Pad: This is very helpful if your eyes aren't as good as they used to be. It looks like a big iPad with different light settings. Place your vinyl on top of the Bright Pad. The cut lines will glow, which will make removing much easier.

Scraper or brayer tools: When working with vinyl, a scraper or brayer tool is very useful. It helps the vinyl stick to the transfer tape and then to the project. When moving vinyl, an old credit card can also be used as a scraper or brayer if you need to.

Vinyl Projects

Here are some ideas for projects with vinyl:

Cricut Bling

Add lots of sparkles to your Cricut with this entertaining craft! Many Cricut crafters slice a sticker of a layout to place on their machine as soon as they receive a fresh cutter. If artistic endeavors aren't your thing, come up with a word or layout that fits your new equipment. Visit Design Space, experiment with some fonts, and create some Cricut Goodies of your own.

Device: Compatible with Cricut Joy, Cricut Explore or Cricut Maker.

What you need:

- Weeding Instruments and Tools
- Transfer Tape.
- Using Measuring Tape
- A scraper tool
- Experimental cut file
- Vinyl in the color of your choice
- Customized grip cutting mat
- Blade with Fine Tip

Instructions:

- Upload the cut file after logging into the Cricut Creation Space.
- Measure the space on your Cricut that will hold your bling. After tapping on the design, you may adjust its size by using the Scale tool in the top toolbar or the arrow located in the bottom right corner of the design.
- Kindly click "Make It." To get the kind of vinyl you require, adjust the cutting material. Using the arrow on the right side of the Cricut to insert your cutting mat, place vinyl on it so that the coloring side is facing up.
- When your mat is ready, look for the Cricut C to start flashing. Then, pull the trigger to start the machine cutting. When your machine stops cutting, click the arrow once again to empty your mat.

- Weed your vinyl, remove any extra vinyl surrounding the logo, and only leave the design on the white paper backing.
- Cut a sheet of transfer tape A little bit larger than your template, After removing the tape from the backrest, set it atop your model. Using the scraper pad, rub the transfer tape's surface, pressing the tape up against the vinyl.
- Raising the vinyl pattern away from the paper's back requires peeling up the transfer tape.
- Position your transfer tape so that the sticky back of the vinyl is where you want your template to go. Use force to ensure the transfer tape is firmly attached to your Cricut by running your scraper tool over the top of it. Carefully remove the transfer tape so that just your template is left!

Coffee and Tea Mugs

Which do you prefer, Tea or Coffee? Mugs are the ideal new addition to any Cricut project, regardless of your team! It's so much pleasure to have a unique mug that represents your individuality. Mugs are also a fantastic homemade present! We provide you with cut files to create a tea or coffee cup, but after completing this project, we highly advise you to let your imagination go wild and truly personalize the mugs you create as gifts! Does the recipient have a favorite sport? Are you a fan of any particular dog breed? Are they your best friend in the world, your granny, or your uncle? Are they still passionate about what they do? These are just a few things to think about when organizing your possible mugs!

Device: Compatible with Cricut Joy, Cricut Explore or Cricut Maker

What you need:

- Transfer tape.
- A scraper tool
- Customized grip cutting mat
- Blade with Fine Tip
- The Mugs
- Using Measuring Tape
- Tea and Coffee Cut Files
- Permanent vinyl
- Weeding Instruments and Tools

Instructions:

- Log into the Cricut Design Space.
- Use the Scale tool in the top toolbar or the arrow located in the bottom right corner of the design to choose the area where you want to bling up your mugs. Then, size the design appropriately.
- Click "Make It." Select the appropriate vinyl type for the cutting content. Using the arrow on the right side of the Cricut to load your slicing mat, place the vinyl onto your cutting mat with the paint facing up.

- Once your mat is loaded, watch for the Cricut C to start blinking. Then, pull the trigger to start your computer cutting. When your computer finished cutting, click the arrow one again to unload your mat.
- Expand your vinyl, remove any extra vinyl from the edges of your layout, and leave only the design on the white paper backing.
- Cut a sheet of transfer tape that is slightly bigger than your template.
- After shaving the backrest, lay the tape over the design. Using the remover pad, rub the transfer tape's surface, pressing the tape up against the vinyl. Raise the vinyl design back from the back of the paper by slicing the transfer tape.
- Carefully position the transfer tape, then set it on your mug. Press the vinyl onto the mug by driving the scraper over the transfer tape.
- Gently remove the tape so that the design remains on your cup. If the vinyl starts to rise, use the scraper to press it down before removing the transfer tape once more.

You can use your mug right away after the 48-hour vinyl setting period! We advise handwashing your cup to preserve the vinyl's longevity! Declare your support for Team Coffee or Team Tea and proudly display it to the world every time you use your gorgeous new mug!

Clipboard with Color Blocks

To connect it to the editing calendar and add regular, weekly, monthly, and annual targets, we made this clipboard for the office. It keeps me focused and serves as a constant reminder to dream big!

Device: Cricut Maker or Explore Project Materials

What you need:

- Transfer tape.
- Tool for braying or scraping
- Using Measuring Tape
- Vinyl in two of your preferred hues
- Customized grip cutting mat
- lanyard
- Large Clipboard Cut File
- Fine Tip Blade with
- Weeding Instruments and Tools

Instructions:

- Log in to Cricut Design Space and upload the Clipboard cut file by following the instructions for SVG uploads.
- Determine the width of your clipboard and adjust the layout to fit. You can accomplish this by tapping on the design and utilizing the Scale tool located in the top toolbar or the arrow located in the bottom right corner of the architecture.
- Kindly click "Make It." Select the appropriate vinyl type for the cutting material. Place the vinyl on your cutting mat with the paint side facing up.
- Press the arrow located on the right side of the Cricut to place your slicing mat into the machine. Once your mat is placed, wait for the Cricut C to blink before pressing the key to initiate the cutting process. When your equipment stops cutting, click the arrow one again to discharge your mat. Repeat this action for the second item in your design.

- Weed your vinyl, remove any extra vinyl from the area around the logo, and leave only the graphics on the white paper backing.
- Cut a piece of tape slightly more than the huge color block piece. After shaving the backing from the transfer tape, place it atop the template. Using the scraper tool or brayer, go over the transfer tape's surface, pressing the tape up against the vinyl. Reposition the vinyl design from the paper's reverse by pealing up the transfer tape.
- Carefully position the transfer tape, then arrange it on your clipboard. Press the vinyl onto the clipboard by passing the scraper over the transfer tape.
- Gently remove the transfer tape, ensuring that the pattern remains on your clipboard by using the scraper to push it back. If the vinyl keeps rising, remove the transfer tape once again.
- Use your new clipboard to prioritize tasks, make to-do lists, and receive personalized reminders that will help you get closer to your amazing objective every day!

Watercolor Wooden Frame

Everywhere you go after purchasing a Cricut, you look for the brand's blank canvases, and the wooden aisle has some amazing options.

Device : Cricut Maker or Explore Weeding Tools are Project Items.

What you need:

- Transfer tape.
- Tool for braying or scraping
- The paintbrush
- Stunning cut file
- Using Measuring Tape
- Wooden photo frame
- Paint
- Vinyl
- Customized grip cutting mat
- Fine Tip Blade

Instructions:

- Paint your image's frame in the first step. Make sure the frame is completely dry before attempting to add vinyl to it.
- After logging in, import the cut file into the Cricut Design Space by following the instructions for Cut File Upload.
- Measure the space where your vinyl will be inserted into the picture frame and adjust the template's size accordingly. You can accomplish this by pressing the template and by using the Scale tool's arrow in the lower right corner of the design located in the top toolbar.
- Kindly click "Make It." Select the appropriate vinyl type for the cutting material. Using the arrow on the right side of the Cricut to install your cutting mat into your Cricut, place the vinyl on your cutting mat with the paint side facing up. Hold off until the Cricut C blinks once.
- Once your mat is attached, press the key to initiate the cutting process on your device. When your Cricut finished cutting, click the arrow one again to unload your mat. Repeat this action for the second item in your design.

- Weed your vinyl, remove any extra vinyl surrounding the logo, and just leave the graphics on the white paper backing.
- Cut a sheet of transfer tape that is slightly larger than your template.
- Place the transfer tape on top of the template after removing the backing. Using the scraper tool or brayer, rub the transfer tape's surface, pressing the tape up against the vinyl. Raising the vinyl design away from the paper's back, shave off excess transfer tape.
- Position the transfer tape on your picture frame where you want your template to be and place it there. Drive the over the transfer tape
- Using a scraper, transfer the vinyl into the image frame. Tear off the transfer tape carefully, preserving the pattern.

Decals for Scrap Nails

What's a crafty girl to do with all those tiny fragments of abandoned vinyl? Why not make vinyl nail decals, of course! Play around with different color schemes and patterns to have fun!

Device: Compatible with Cricut Joy, Cricut Explore or Cricut Ma

What you need:

- Customized grip cutting mat
- lucid nail varnish
- Vinyl remnants
- Blade with Fine Tip

Instructions:

- Choose a form from Cricut Design Space after logging in. You can use hearts, triangles, squares, and other common forms under the Shape tool for free.
- Create the shape you want for your nail decals. Depending on the nail's size, we suggest between 0.15 and 0.5 inches.
- Kindly click "Make It." To get the kind of vinyl you require, modify the slicing material.
- To put your slicing mat into your Cricut, lie vinyl on your cutting mat with the paint side facing up. Use the arrow located on the right side of the Cricut.
- When your mat is loaded and the Cricut C starts blinking, pull the trigger to initiate the cutting process. When your gadget stops cutting, click the arrow once again to empty your mat.

- Weed your vinyl, cutting off any extra material surrounding the image, and leaving only the design on the white paper backing.
- Gently remove the decals from the paper backing and apply them to your nails.

BOOK 6:
HANDMADE IRON-ON AND HEAT TRANSFER VINYL (HTV)

The ideal material for cutting is HTV. We think that having the ability to create your own unique tees is well worth the cost of a Cricut! But HTV may be used for so much more than shirts.

Heat Transfer Vinyl, HTV, and Iron-On are all different titles for the same material! Although the terms should be used interchangeably, don't be alarmed if you see a crafter switching between terms.

Practical Techniques for HTV Work

For cutting HTV and other common materials including vinyl, cardstock, scrapbook paper, and more, this is the recommended blade. Blade with a Fine Tip for Cutting.

Standard grip cutting pad: A typical grip-cutting mat has the proper grip to make your HTV safe when cutting.

Weeding tools: Using weeding tools, you can remove the HTV "negative space" from your template and the area around it. It is quite helpful in weeding small lettering and intricate designs. Additionally, vinyl and paper weeding supplies are available.

Cricut Bright Pad: If your eyesight is declining, a Cricut Bright Pad can be of great assistance. It has multiple illumination settings and appears to be a large iPad. Your weeding will be much smoother if you place your HTV over the top of the Bright Pad, which will accentuate your cut lines.

Brayer tools: Having a brayer tool on hand is really helpful when

HTV Work: We enjoy running the brayer over the top of our build in between each press. We believe it also seeks to ensure that our HTV is pressed into and adheres to the materials of anything we adhere to.

Iron-On Protective Sheet: You can prevent heat damage to your HTV by using iron-on protective sheets with a nonstick surface. Additionally, they help to distribute the heat from your iron, heat press, or Easy Press more evenly.

There are four sizes of the Cricut Easy Press: the smallest is the itty bitty Easy Press Mini, and the largest is the 12 to 10-inch press, which is perfect for larger projects.

There are four sizes available for the Cricut Easy Press. To assist you achieve flawless outcomes, heat presses and Easy Presses also have pressure, heat signatures, and dependable temperature control.

Easy Press Mat: this practical little mat is designed to do more than just protect the work area from heat (but it accomplishes that too!). It includes a foil surface that reflects heat and a unique inner liner that wicks moisture to provide the project clean, dry heat. For amazing HTV results, the soft protective barrier bottom also aids in locking layers together!

Stylish Sweatshirt

Visit the store, select your preferred blank sweatshirt, and create your own! Not a fan of sweatshirts? Try this on a T-shirt, a tank top, or even a tote bag filled with art supplies!

Device: Compatible with Cricut Joy, Cricut Explore or Cricut Maker Project

What you need:

To protect your work surface, use a towel or an Easy Press Mat.

- Creative cut file
- Brayer and the iron-on protective film are optional.
- Vinyl for heat transfer in your preferred hues
- Customized grip cutting mat
- blank sweater
- Using Measuring Tape
- Fine Tip Blade
- Weeding Instruments and Tools
- Cricut Iron or Easy Press

Instructions:

- Import the "Crafty" cut file after logging into the Cricut Design Space. To adjust each cut-out file piece to the HTV color you're using, click on it.
- Weigh your sweater at the desired style point. The template can be resized by tapping on it and use the Sizing tool in the top toolbar or the arrow located in the bottom right corner of the design.

Pro Tip

Click the "Templates" icon in Design Space. A menu appears with a variety of items you could find useful for your Cricut. Prior to cutting it out, select the one that most closely resembles the space you're using, then check how your template appears on that piece.

- Kindly click "Make It." Under each cutting mat, press the mirrored slider located on the left side of the screen. As you follow the on-screen instructions, modify the cutting material to fit the HTV form you are using.
- After placing your iron-on with the color side facing downwards on the cutting surface, load your cutting mat into the Cricut using the arrow located on its right side. Once your mat is attached and the Cricut C starts blinking, press the key to initiate the cutting process. When your machine stops cutting, click the arrow one again to release the mat. Do this for every hue of HTV.

- Weed your HTV, removing the covering surrounding the logo and replacing it with just the graphic on the translucent plastic backing.
- Cut away enough of the clear plastic backing around the letters so that you can position your logo on the sweatshirt without anything getting in the way. To add the iron-on style to the fabric used to make your sweatshirt, follow the instructions.
- Using the iron-on protective sheet is optional, but it gives the template an additional degree of security. We particularly enjoy forcing the vinyl through the shirt fibers between presses with the HTV brayer tool.
- Gently remove the clear plastic lining to reveal your beautifully crafted hoodie!

Handmade Napkins

Is there a party or other event planned? Adding HTV on paper napkins is a genius technique to elevate them to a whole new level for retail locations! Customize ceremony napkins by cutting them into tassels or adding autographs, a pattern inspired by your party theme, include your birthday number, or just refer to all fun occasions as "Celebrations." You'll get a lot of use out of it, and it's such an easy and fun DIY! Put on your thinking cap and brainstorm celebrations for Mother's Day, Father's Day, Christmas, New Year's Eve, Easter, July Fourth, birthdays, marriages, retirements, baby showers, and more!

Device: Cricut Joy-compatible Cricut Maker or Cricut Explore

What you need:

- Weeding Instruments and Tools
- Cricut Iron or Easy Press
- Using Measuring Tape
- Pap napkins
- Customized grip cutting mat
- To protect your work surface, use a towel or an Easy Press Mat.
- Celebrate the cut file—or create one yourself!
- Shiny iron-on
- Fine Tip Blade

Instructions:

- Use the Cut File Upload instructions to upload the "Celebrate" cut file after logging into the Cricut Design Room.
- Determine the placement of your napkin and the pattern. The design can be resized by tapping on the layout or by utilizing the Sizing tool in the top toolbar, the arrow that shows in the lower right corner of the design, or both. Click Duplicate to make a copy of the screenshot showing how many napkins you truly want to customize.
- Kindly click "Make It." Under the cutting board, on the right side of the page, press the mirror lever. As you follow the on-screen instructions, modify the

cutting material to fit the HTV form you are using. Using the arrow on the right side of the Cricut, place your iron-on on the cutting mat with the color side down, then load the cutting mat into the machine. After mounting your mat, wait for the Cricut C to blink before pulling the trigger to start cutting. When your equipment stops cutting, click the arrow one again to discharge your mat.

- Weed the iron-on and cut it around the logo, leaving only the template on the clear plastic backing.
- Iron your pattern onto each napkin by following the instructions to add paper or cardstock to the type of iron-on you're using. Leave the logo on the napkin and remove the plastic after it cools down enough to touch.

Handmade Pillowcase

Pillowcases create a large, exquisite blank canvas that may be personalized in a myriad of ways, including initials, titles, quotes, sayings, and your favorite fictional characters or animals! Also, we've employed a flocke

Device: Cricut Maker or Explore Tools for the Project: Cricut

What you need:

- Easy Press or Iron
- Cut File: Traveling Directly to Dreamland
- To protect your work surface, use a towel or an Easy Press Mat.
- HTV in the hues of your choice
- Customized grip cutting mat
- Using Measuring Tape
- Unused pillowcase
- Fine Tip Blade
- Weeding Instruments and Tools

Instructions:

- Upload the cut file by logging in to the Cricut Modeling Space and following the Cut File Upload instructions. To adjust the cut out file to the HTV color you are using, press on each piece.
- Tap your pillowcase to locate the pattern. Use the Sizing feature in the top toolbar or the arrow in the bottom right corner to resize the design.
- Click "Make It." Press the mirror lever located beneath the cutting mat on the left side of the screen. As you adhere to the on-screen instructions, set the cutting material to the HTV shape you are using. After positioning your iron-on on the cutting board with the colored side facing downward, load your cutting mat into the Cricut using the arrow located on its right side. After mounting your mat, wait for the Cricut C to blink before pulling the trigger to start cutting. When your equipment stops cutting, click the arrow one again to discharge your mat. Say this again for every HTV color.

- Weed your HTV, removing the material surrounding the logo and replacing it with simply the design and a translucent plastic backdrop.
- Adhere to the instructions for securing the iron-on form on the item that will be used to make your pillowcase.
- Using the iron-on protective sheet is optional, but it gives the template an additional degree of security. We thoroughly like driving the vinyl through the pillowcase fibers between each press utilizing the HTV brayer process.
- The design underneath is revealed by cutting the clear plastic lining.

Zippered Pouch for Coloring

Do you adore the color green? Adult coloring books, which explained to tweens, teens, and adults why youngsters love coloring so much, were incredibly popular a few years ago. It's quite enjoyable and calming! A whole new level of coloring is introduced in this project! Our coloring canvas is a zippered fabric pouch, on which we draw our design using black HTV and paint it with fabric markers. This project is easy to do and fun for all ages! What other supplies do you use to color canvases? Pillowcases, baseball caps, T-shirts, sweatshirts, tote bags, and much more! There're still so many choices!

Device: Compatible with Cricut Joy, Cricut Explore or Cricut Maker Project

What you need:

- Black HTV
- Cricut Iron or Easy Press
- Customized grip cutting mat
- Fine Tip Blade
- To protect your work surface, use a towel or an Easy Press Mat.
- Textile markers
- Weeding Instruments and Tools
- Cactus cutting file
- Measuring Tape
- Brayer and the iron-on protective film are optional.

Instructions:

- Log in to the Cricut Design Space and upload the Stay Sharp cactus cut file by following the instructions for Cut File Upload.
- Use the Sizing function in the top toolbar or the arrow in the template's bottom right corner to scale the design.
- Kindly click "Make It." Press the mirror lever located beneath the cutting board on the left side of the screen. As you follow the on-screen instructions, adjust the cutting material to the HTV form you are now using. After positioning your iron-on on the cutting mat with the colored side facing downward, attach the

slicing mat into the Cricut using the arrow on the right hand of the device. Once your mat is mounted, wait for the Cricut C to flash before clicking the key to initiate the cutting process. When your machine stops cutting, click the arrow one again to release the mat.

- Weed your HTV, removing the covering surrounding the logo and replacing it with just the graphic on the translucent plastic backing.
- Attach the iron-on style to the fabric that will be used to make your zippered pouch by following the instructions.
- Using the iron-on protective sheet is optional, but it gives the template an additional degree of security. We truly enjoy forcing the vinyl into the bag's fibers with each press using the HTV brayer tool.
- The design underneath is revealed by cutting the clear plastic lining. The color in your zippered pouch. When sketching, we think of putting a piece of cardstock inside the zippered pouch so that the ink doesn't leak out the opposite side.

Stuff your lovely zipped pouch full of your favorite things, like lip balm, washi tape, pencils in your favorite colors, and more!

BOOK 7:
PAPER PROJECTS

Paper is a great material to start with when learning how to use your Cricut because it is one of the cheapest materials available. A lot of people who make cards buy Cricuts to help them take their card-making skills to the next level, never realizing that it would open up a world of opportunities for the rest of their craft lives!

Here are some Ideas for projects on "paper":

Different types of paper, finishes, and weights can all be cut with the Cricut. At the beginning of this book, you can find a complete list of the paper types that the Cricut Maker and Cricut Explore can cut.

These types of paper have been used in many projects:

- Cards with glitter
- Paper for scrapbooks
- Regular playing cards
- Paper crepe
- Paper Vellum
- Boxes of cereal
- Paper for building
- A poster board
- Photographs

What you need to know

Paper Weight: You must select the appropriate weight of paper when cutting cards with your Cricut Maker or using the custom setting on the Cricut. When 500 sheets of paper were made, they weighed 11 or 12 pounds before being cut to 8.5-inch sizes..

Weeding: Weeding is the process of cutting away the extra space around your design, leaving only the design on the cutting mat.

Print and Cut: Print and Cut is a tool in Cricut Design Space that allows you to print out a design using your home printer and then have your Cricut cut it out for you.

Scoring: Scoring means making a mark on the paper, generally in the shape of a line, so it can fold easily and cleanly along the line.

Quilling: Quilling means making a coil shape out of paper by winding it around a quill.

Fine-tip cutting blade: This is the best blade for cutting paper and most other common materials, like iron-on, cardboard, scrapbook paper, and more. To find out what blades you need for different types of material, look at the list of materials at the beginning of the book.

LightGrip cutting mat: A LightGrip cutting mat has the right grip to keep your paper safe while you cut and to preserve its shape when you try to remove it from the mat.

Weeding tools: Weeding tools help you move the unwanted space from around your design. This would be very helpful when working with paper and making more complicated designs, like for shadowboxes.

Brayer tools: I love using a brayer to press the paper down evenly on the LightGrip cutting mat. That way, the paper doesn't move around while you cut.

Paper Projects

Gift tags that say "THANK YOU" and "HANDMADE WITH LOVE"

Once you have a Cricut, you'll find that you can make a lot of things that you used to buy, like gift tags! To make pretty gift tags, use your Cricut to cut out craft paper, old calendars, cards, and other pretty colored paper. If you want to make your Cricut and printer work together, you can use plain white cardstock and the Print and Cut tool, which is what we're going to do in this project.

What you need:

- Gift Tag Cut Files with "Thank You" and "Handmade With Love"
- Cards that are white
- Color Printer
- A cutting mat with LightGrip
- Fine Tip Blade

Instructions:

- Open Cricut Design Space and upload the Gift Tag cut file
- Make your design 9.25 inches wide by clicking on it and using the Size tool in the top toolbar or the arrow that shows in the bottom right corner of the design.
- Click "Make It". Do what the screen tells you to do. You'll start by using your printer to make the gift tags Then, using the arrow buttons on the right side of the cutting machine, you will select your cutting material, place your printed gift tags on the cutting mat, and load it into the machine. When your mat is ready to cut, look for the Cricut C to start flashing. Press the button, and your machine will begin cutting. Press the arrow again when your machine is done cutting, and your mat will come off.

Note: If your Cricut doesn't start cutting right away, don't worry. There will likely be a light that turns on near the blade. The light will move the mat back and forth across your paper. It is your Cricut looking for the black line to tell it where to cut.

Carefully remove the gift tags from the cutting mat. You can use them now!

Lights In A Sleepy Village

With these simple house lights, you can make a beautiful, glowing winter scene. When lit with a battery-powered light, these paper houses look beautiful in any setting.

As a mantle or as the center of a table. You can make the tiny town of your dreams with just one cut file that lets you make houses of different sizes and colors.

What you need:

- Cut File for Sleepy Village
- Cardstock in various sizes and colors
- A cutting mat with LightGrip
- Blade with a Fine Tip
- A score pen or wheel
- Dots of Glue or Glue
- Candles that run on batteries

Instructions:

- Open Cricut Design Space and add the Sleepy Village cut file by following the guidelines on page 28 of this manual.
- Select the score line by clicking the Shapes button in the right-hand tool bar. In all the places shown in the picture, add score lines. You will need your paper to be able to fold in these places so that you can make your houses. Select the house and all of the score lines, then click Attach.
- To make as many houses as you want, click the "Duplicate" button. To open up the size percentage, click the Lock button. Change the sizes of the houses by making some taller and thinner, some shorter and wider, and some bigger and smaller. Make sure you know what size paper and cutting mats you have so that each house can fit on the paper.
- Click "Make It." Do what the screen tells you to do. Put the paper on the cutting mat and then put the scoring stylus or wheel into the machine. Using the direction buttons on the right side of the machine, insert your mat into the machine. Once your mat is added, wait for the Cricut C to flash. Then press the

button, and your machine will start cutting and scoring. Press the arrow again when your machine is done cutting, and your mat will come off.

- Fold your paper at each score line once all of your houses have been cut. To keep the tabs in place, use glue or Glue Dots.
- For a beautiful, glowing, sleepy town, put at least one battery-powered candle inside each house.

Picture cards for Father's Day and Mother's Day

Device: The Cricut Maker or the Cricut Explore

The right picture can take you back to a certain place or time. You will learn how to make a photo card and envelope with this project. This can be used as a Mother's Day or Father's Day card. You can use this cut file to make photo cards for any holiday or special occasion once you know the basics. Just add your own extra embellishments. As well as Christmas and Valentine's Day, photo cards are great for birthdays, weddings, grads, baby shower thank-you cards, and more!

What you need:

- Pic card cutting file
  - Cut file envelope
  - A print and cut file with Mother's Day decorations
  - Print and cut file for Father's Day gifts
  - White paper 8.5 x 11 inches
  - 3 pieces of 12x12-inch paper in the colors or patterns of your choice
  - Color Printer
  - A cutting mat with LightGrip
  - Fine Tip Blade
  - Scoring pen or scoring blade
  - Glue Sticks
  - Your favorite picture

Instructions:

- Open Cricut Design Space and follow the steps on page 28 of this book to add the photo card, envelope, and Mother's Day or Father's Day cut files. Remember to save the Mother's Day and Father's Day parts as a Print and Cut file.
- Make the card 5 inches wide. Round the corners of the square picture backer so that it is 4 inches wide. Make the envelope 11.75 inches tall. Cut the Mother's Day and Father's Day parts to the sizes you want to use on your card.
- Take your envelope and envelope lining off by clicking the "Detach" button on the right-hand toolbar. Make score lines on the card, envelope, and envelope

liner. To add a score line, click on the Shapes tool in the left menu. Pick out the Score Line. Plan where you want the score to go on the card or envelope. Then, select the score line and the thing you want to attach it to. Finally, click the Attach button on the right-hand toolbar. You can use the "Align" button in the top menu to center your score line on the card.

- Click "Make It." Do what the screen tells you to do. You'll start by using your printer to print your Mother's Day or Father's Day decorations.
- Then, using the arrow buttons on the right side of the machine, you will select your cutting material, place your printed pages on the cutting mat, and load it into the machine. When your mat is ready to cut, look for the Cricut C to start flashing. Press the button, and your machine will begin cutting. Press the arrow again when your machine is done cutting, and your mat will come off.

Note: If your Cricut doesn't start cutting right away, don't worry. There will likely be a light that turns on near the blade. The mat will move as the light goes back and forth over your

Write on paper. It is your Cricut looking for the black line to tell it where to cut.

- After cutting all of your pieces, fold each one with a score line along the score line. The envelope divider should then be adhered to the interior of the envelope with Glue Dots, and the envelope flaps should then be sealed. Then, put the Father's Day or Mother's Day parts of your card on the front. Stick a picture inside the card's hole, then attach a picture backing with Glue Dots to keep it in place.
- This is a lovely picture card for Mother's or Father's Day in the making! Make the card even more unique by using front-of-card features that are related to hobbies or things the recipient is interested in.

Party Hats With Pom-Poms

When you have a Cricut, party planning is so much more fun because you can make Anything!

Put it on with iron. This project shows you how to make simple party hats with a pom-pom or felt ball on top! Because there is such a wide variety of scrapbook paper available at the craft, the possibilities that can be achieved with these are truly endless. Can't seem to settle on a winning design? Before you put the party hats together, choose an exciting color of craft paper, cut some iron-on or vinyl into shapes that correspond with your theme, and adhere those shapes to the paper.

What you need:

- Cut file for a party hat
- A cutting mat with LightGrip
- Fun 12x12-inch scrapbook paper (1 piece per hat) in fun colors and designs
- Fine Tip Blade
- Hot glue sticks and Glue Gun
- Balls of felt or pom-poms
- Punch a hole
- Either yarn, string, or rope
- Stipes
- Brayer (optional)

Instructions:

- Open Cricut Design Space and add the Party Hat cut file
- Make the cut file 11.5 inches wide. You can do this by clicking on the picture and then using the size boxes in the tool bar at the top of Cricut Design Space.
- Click "Make It". Do what the screen tells you to do. Choose your cutting machine, place your scrapbook paper on the cutting mat, and put it into the machine using the arrow buttons on the right side of the machine. When your mat is ready to cut, look for the Cricut C to start flashing. Press the button, and your machine will begin cutting. Once you press the button, your machine will

start the cutting process. When the cutting process on your machine is complete, you can remove the mat by pressing the arrow button once more.

- Gently remove the scrapbook paper from the cutting mat. Make the scrapbook into the shape of a party hat by rolling it up. Then, glue the edges of the papers together where they meet to keep the book shut. Put a small amount of hot glue on your pom-pom or felt ball and stick it on top of the hat.

- Punch holes near the bottom of both sides of your party hat with your hole punch. Cut yarn, string, or elastic into the right sizes to make chin straps for the people at your party. To make chin straps, tie the yarn through the holes you just made.

- Wearing your party hats to your next big event will be a ton of fun!

Sloth Sleep Mask

This adorable personalized sleep mask is perfect for sleep parties to wear. Make a whole family of drowsy sloth sleep masks and gift them to everyone you care about!

Device: Cricut Maker

What you need:

- Fine tip Blade
- Heat conversion vinyl
- Layer of Protection Cricut Iron-On
- Use a piece of cloth measuring 10 by 12 inches for the front of your mask.
- Cricut Easy Press or Iron
- The shield's back was made of a 10 x 12 inch piece of cloth
- A 12-inch long black elastic piece
- matching-colored thread
- Scraps
- Wonder Clips or Pins
- Clothes Needle
- The Sloth Sleep Mask cut file
- Fabric Grip Adhesive Cutting Pad
- Normal grip for a cutting mat
- Cricut Rotary Blade

Instructions:

- Import the cut files for the Sloth Sleep Mask after logging into the Cricut Design Space.
- Scale the design to 8.5 inches in height by tapping on the layout or by using the Size function in the top toolbar or the arrow in the lower right corner of the design.
- Kindly click "Make It." The sleep mask-shaped sections can be cut out of fabric by following the instructions for cutting each sleeping mask piece, loading the necessary mats, slicing the blade, and cutting the Fabric Grip sticky slicing mat and the rotating saw.

- The sloth face parts can be removed from the HTV by using the regular grip cutting pad and fine-tip cutter (please make sure your HTV is loaded with the glossy colored side down).
- Fill your slicing mat with each item using the arrow on the right side of your Cricut, select the required material from the drop-down menu, and then mount the cutting unit. Once your mat is loaded, look for the Cricut C to start blinking. Then, click the trigger to start your device. When your Cricut stops cutting, click the arrow once more to offload your mat. Repeat for each material you are cutting.
- After you've cut all the bits, it's time to iron the forms to the front of your sleep mask fabric. It needs to be stacked, which can be difficult if the iron-on refuses to burn. We find that using the Cricut Iron-On Protective Mat makes blending so much easier.
- First, add the hairline and eye patches of the sloth, followed by the nose, the black eye sections, the white-eye dots, and the whites of the eyes.
- It's time to start sewing! Attach your elastic to the back flannel portion of the sleep mask. Allow the elastic to extend the mask's edge by ½ inch on each foot.
- A "sleep mask sandwich" is what you want to create first. The side of the fleece with the elastic attached should be facing up. Place your nose and eyes down and the front of your facemask on top of it. Since iron-on has been applied to the mask's face, we advise using wonder clips to avoid poking a hole in the mask and/or being careful where you put your pins.
- Using a ¼-inch seam allowance, stitch all the way around the outside seam of your sleep mask, being careful to leave a 1-inch or wider opening so that you can turn it right side out.
- Turn the right side of the mask out, press it in place (using the iron-on shielding sheet to help you squeeze the sloth's face), and use a needle and thread to stitch the hole you made in the right side of the mask to transform it.

You've got it there, too! Sloth Has A Cute Sleep Mask! Wear it for the guaranteed sloth sleep!

Bandana with Animal Collar

The Animal Collar Bandana makes ideal gifts for dog owners or animal enthusiasts.

Device: Easy Press or Cricut Iron

What you need:

- Sewing machine
- Cutters
- Rotary Blade Cricut
- Imaginary pins or clips
- Matching colored thread.
- Adhesive Fabric Grip cutting mat
- Bandana Cut File for Over-the-Collar Pets

Instructions:

- import the Pet Bandana cut file after logging into the Cricut Design Space.
- Determine the weight of your pet's collar by placing your hand where the bandana wants you to rest. The region at the bottom of the triangle (the arrow in the picture between the two arrows) will be resized to a specific size when you press the cut file. Press the Duplication button to make the second piece the same size.
- Kindly click "Make It." Adhere to the guidelines to pick the type of fabric you're using. Put the cloth on the Fabric Grip pad. Click the blinking Cricut C after using the arrow button on the Cricut Maker to mount your slicing mat. Proceed with the second piece of material.
- Remove the cut cloth from the cutting pad. Next, we want to fold the label ends over so that there aren't any exposed cloth edges when we slide the bandana over the collar. To ensure that the triangle's base and tip meet, fold the tab on top. Use your Easy Press or iron to press the fold into place after folding once more for a neat, tidy trim. Tabs 1 and 2 should be repeated on all cloth bits.
- Next, align the corners of both pieces of your bandana, pressing the printed side of the garment into the center. Thread over the bandana's top lip by using a ¼-inch seam allowance. Next, stitch from the base of your hemmed tab all the way

down to the bottom of the triangle and back up to the base of the second hemmed tab. To feed the collar through the right-side bandana, make sure to leave the hemmed tabs open.

- Make sure all of your corners are pushed out by flipping out your bandana on your right side. Make sure your scarf has neat, vibrant corners by ironing it.
- Now you have a cute pet bandana that you can wear over your collar! Put the bandana around your pet's neck after feeding it through the collar.

BOOK 8:
DIY PROJECTS AND INFUSIBLE INK

Infusible Paint, Circuit's sublimation edition, is fantastic! At the moment this book is being written, there are two ways of using Infusible Ink.

Infusible Ink is Cricut-specific ink for compatible materials and cutting machines. Infusible Ink Transfer Sheets and Infusible Ink Pens & Markers are the two main methods for using infusible ink.

Infusible Ink Transfer Sheets:

Materials Required:

- Infusible Ink Transfer Sheets: Cricut-compatible ink sheets.
- Cricut blanks (T-shirts, tote bags, coasters, etc.) made of at least 50% polyester work best with Infusible Ink. Materials must withstand heat and pressure during the transfer process because the ink is infused into them.

Cutting Machine: Cricut Explore Air 2 or Maker.

Heat Press or EasyPress: A heat press or EasyPress transfers ink from the transfer sheet to the base material.

Design: Use Cricut Design Space or another compatible design software to design.

- Cut the design from the Infusible Ink Transfer Sheet with your Cricut.
- Ready Base Material: Pre-heat the base material to remove wrinkles and moisture.
- Transfer: Lay the cut Infusible Ink design face-down on the base. Attach the design with heat-resistant tape.
- Apply Heat: Use a heat press or EasyPress at the recommended temperature and time for your Infusible Ink and material. Heat and pressure will transfer ink to the material, creating a vibrant, permanent design.

Infusible Ink Markers & Pens:

Materials needed:

Infusible Ink Pens and Markers: Infusible ink is used in these pens and markers.

- Compatible Paper: Laser copy paper works best.
- Heat-resistant tape: To hold the design during transfer.
- EasyPress Mat: A heat-resistant, firm transfer surface.
- Cricut Cutting Machine: Optional for cutting out your design after drawing.

Steps:

Design: Draw or design on compatible paper with Infusible Ink Pens or Markers.

Preheat base material (like a T-shirt) with an EasyPress to remove wrinkles and moisture.

Secure Design: Secure the drawing face-down on the preheated base material with heat-resistant tape to prevent movement during transfer.

Apply Heat: Use an EasyPress machine on an EasyPress Mat at the recommended temperature and time for your Infusible Ink pens/markers and material. Heat and pressure will transfer ink to the material, creating a vibrant, durable design.

Projects with Infusible Ink

Here are the steps for making DIY projects with Infusible Ink:

Customized T-Shirts

- Design: Use Cricut Design Space or compatible software to design.
- Cut: Cut Infusible Ink Transfer Sheets with a Cricut.
- Prep T-shirt: To remove wrinkles and moisture, pre-heat your polyester-blend T-shirt.
- Transfer the cut Infusible Ink design to the T-shirt face-down. Wrap it in heat-resistant tape.
- Use a heat press at the recommended temperature and time. Put even pressure on the shirt to transfer ink.
- Peel and Cool: Before removing the transfer sheet, allow the T-shirt to cool. Your design is permanently woven into the fabric.

Tote Bags:

- Infusible Ink Transfer Sheets are used to cut out your design.
- To remove wrinkles and moisture, preheat your polyester-blend tote bag.
- Transfer: Using heat-resistant tape, attach the design to the tote bag.
- Heat Press: Transfer the design to the tote bag using a heat press at the recommended temperature and time.
- Before removing the transfer sheet, let the bag cool. Peel and cool. Your personalized tote bag is ready.

Coasters:

- Infusible Ink Transfer Sheets are used to cut coaster-sized designs.
- Preheat Infusible Ink-compatible coasters.
- Transfer: Heat-resistant tape is used to secure the design to the coasters.
- Heat Press: Transfer the design to coasters using a heat press at the recommended temperature and time.
- Allow the coasters to cool before removing the transfer sheet. Peel and cool. Your customized coasters are done.

Mugs:

- Create your design on laser copy paper using Infusible Ink Pens or Markers.
- Wrap Mug: Wrap design paper around mug with heat-resistant tape.
- Heat Press: Transfer the design to the mug using a heat press at the recommended temperature and time.
- Peel the paper after letting the mug cool completely. Your personalized mug is dishwasher and microwave safe.

Keychains:

- Create your design on laser copy paper using Infusible Ink Pens or Markers.
- Cutting: Cut the paper keychain shape.
- Prepare Keychain: Preheat Infusible Ink keychain blanks.
- Transfer: Use heat-resistant tape to adhere the paper design to the keychain blank.
- Heat Press: Transfer the design to the keychain using a heat press at the recommended temperature and time.
- Peel and Cool: Before removing the paper, let the keychain cool. Your customized keychain is ready.

Baby Onesies:

- Infusible Ink Transfer Sheets are used to cut out your design.
- Prepare Onesie: To remove wrinkles and moisture, preheat the polyester-blend baby onesie.
- Transfer: Using heat-resistant tape, attach the design to the onesie.
- Use a heat press at the recommended temperature and time to transfer the design to the onesie.
- Peel the transfer sheet after letting the onesie cool. Your personalized baby onesie is done.

Mouse Pads:

- Infusible Ink Transfer Sheets are used to cut out your design.
- Preheat compatible mouse pad to remove wrinkles and moisture.
- Transfer: Using heat-resistant tape, attach the design to the mouse pad.
- Heat Press: Transfer the design to the mouse pad using a heat press at the recommended temperature and time.
- Peel and cool before removing the transfer sheet. Your customized mouse pad is ready.

Puzzles:

- Design and cut your puzzle from Infusible Ink Transfer Sheets.
- To remove wrinkles and moisture from the puzzle, preheat it.
- Transfer: Using heat-resistant tape, attach the design to the puzzle.
- Heat Press: Transfer the design to the puzzle using a heat press at the recommended temperature and time.
- Peel and Cool: Before removing the transfer sheet, let the puzzle cool. Your custom puzzle is ready.

Pillow Covers:

- Infusible Ink Transfer Sheets are used to cut out your design.
- Pillow Cover Prep: Heat the polyester-blend pillow cover to remove wrinkles and moisture.
- Transfer: Use heat-resistant tape to secure the design to the pillow cover.
- Heat Press: Transfer the design to the pillow cover using a heat press at the recommended temperature and time.
- Cool and Peel: Before removing the transfer sheet, let the pillow cover cool. Finished personalizing your pillow cover.

Drink Cozies:

- Infusible Ink Transfer Sheets are used to cut out your design.
- Prepare Cozy: Preheat the Infusible Ink drink cozy.
- Transfer: Using heat-resistant tape, adhere the design to the cozy.
- Heat Press: Transfer the design to the cozy using a heat press at the recommended temperature and time.
- Peel the transfer sheet after letting the cozy cool. Your personalized drink cozy is ready.

The Cricut Knife Blade unlocked the way to an entirely new universe of craft potential, particularly for home

BOOK 9:
SPECIAL MATERIALS

Here are the steps for making Cricut Maker projects using special materials like engraving on bracelets, making personalized phone cases, etching glass, and using the Foil Quill tool to make a leather lip balm holder:

Text-Engraved Bracelet:

Materials:

- Cricut Engraving Tip
- Bracelet Bending Bar Blank
- Strong grip cutting mat
- Painter's or masking tape
- Optional Metal Stamp Enamel Marker

Steps:

- Design: Insert text into Cricut Design Space and choose Engrave mode for Linetype. Select your font and size.
- Resize your text to fit the bracelet. For bracelet placement, note the design center.
- Bracelet: Lay the bracelet down on the cutting mat and tape it down. In your Cricut machine, place the mat inside.
- In Cricut Design Space, insert the Cricut Engraving Tip and begin engraving. Remove the bracelet from the mat after engraving.
- Finish: Bend the bracelet with the bending bar. An optional Metal Stamp Enamel Marker can clean up the engraved lines.

Customized Pop Socket Covers:

Materials:

- Sharp-bladed Cricut machine
- Compact pop-socket phone
- Printable vinyl or stickers
- For cutting, use a Pop Socket File.
- Personalized grip cutting mat

Steps:

- Designer: Upload Pop Socket Covers to Cricut Design Space. Size the designs to fit your pop socket.
- Print and Cut: Print designs on vinyl or stickers. Cut the designs on the printed sheet using your Cricut machine on the personalized cutting mat.
- Peel off the stickers' backing and stick them to your phone's pop socket. Press down to ensure adhesion.

Handmade Wine Glasses with Etched Design:

Materials:

- Vinyl stencil
- Wine Glass
- Etching cream
- Paint paste
- Paintbrush
- The measurement band
- Weeding tools
- Transfer tape

Steps:

- Clean and dry the wine glass with soap and water.
- Design: Upload the design to Cricut Design Space. Adjust the wine glass design size and position.
- Cut Vinyl Stencil: Cut the design. Remove excess vinyl to reveal the design.
- Transfer: Apply vinyl stencil to wine glass using transfer tape. Apply it smoothly without air bubbles.
- Use a thin layer of etching cream inside the stencil. Follow the etching cream packaging instructions for the required time. Wash off the etching cream and remove the stencil to see the design.

Foil Quill Fox Leather Lip Balm Holder:

Materials:

- Foil Quill
- Faux leather
- Cut File Lip Balm Holder
- Sewing machine and thread
- Keychain/carabiner
- Scissors

Steps:

- Warm up Foil Quill for 5 minutes. Select the Cricut machine's connector and insert the Foil Quill into the pen holder.
- Design: Upload Lip Balm Holder cut file to Cricut Design Space. Scale the design for faux leather.
- Foil: Cover the cut mat's faux leather with foil. Start Foil Quill to foil the leather design.
- Using your Cricut machine, cut the lip balm holders from faux leather after foiling.
- Attach the keychain or carabiner to one lip balm holder end. Stitch the leather edges with a sewing machine. Remove excess thread with scissors.

Working on these projects requires following all Cricut machine and tool safety instructions. Have fun crafting!

BOOK 10:
ADVANCED CRICUT TECHNIQUES

dvanced Cricut techniques let you use many materials and create intricate, textured designs. Here are some advanced material techniques, such as heat transfer on special fabrics and surfaces and layering materials for textured designs:

Unique Fabrics and Surfaces Heat Transfer:

Materials:

- Special fabrics (burlap, canvas, faux leather)
- Vinyl heat-transfer
- With a fine-point blade, the Cricut Cutting Machine
- Weeding tools
- EasyPress machine or heat press

Steps:

- Design: Make or choose a heat transfer design. Mirror the design before cutting.
- Cut the mirrored design with your Cricut machine on the heat-transfer vinyl mat.
- Weed: Using weeding tools, carefully remove the extra vinyl until the carrier sheet has the desired design.
- To remove wrinkles and moisture, preheat the special fabric. Place it on the EasyPress mat or heat press.
- Transfer: Place the weeded design on fabric. Use Teflon or parchment paper. To transfer the design to the fabric, use a heat press or EasyPress machine set to the right temperature and time.
- Let the fabric cool before gently peeling it off the carrier sheet. The heat-transfer vinyl should permanently adhere to the unique fabric, resulting in a customized design.

Layering Materials for Textured Design:

Materials:

- Various materials
- With a fine-point blade, the Cricut Cutting Machine
- Transfer Tape Vinyl
- Foam or adhesive squares for paper
- Fabric glue
- Foil Quill

Steps:

- Multi-layer design: Use different materials and colors for each layer in Cricut Design Space.
- Cut: Place each material on the cutting mat one at a time, then use your Cricut machine to cut the corresponding layers.
- Weed Vinyl: Use weeding tools to remove excess vinyl, leaving the design elements.
- Assemble (for Paper): Use adhesive or foam squares to stack paper layers for 3D effect. Put glue on the back of each layer and stack carefully.
- Vinyl Layer Transfer: Apply vinyl layers to the desired surface using transfer tape. One layer at a time, aligning.
- To create a textured fabric design, apply fabric glue to the back of fabric layers and carefully position them on the base fabric.
- Foil Quill (for Foil): Add intricate foil designs to other materials with the foil quill tool. To foil intricate elements, follow the foil quill instructions.
- Experiment with materials, colors, and textures to create stunning and textured designs with your Cricut machine. To get the best results, follow material and technique guidelines.

Techniques for Embossing and Debossing:

Materials:

- Debossing tip for Cricut Cuttlebug or Maker
- Cuttlebug embossing folders

Steps to use cardstock or paper:

- Design: Choose or create a Cricut Design Space design. Embossing and debossing techniques are good for intricate designs.
- Cut or Deboss: For the Cricut Cuttlebug, insert the cardstock or paper into the embossing folder and turn on the machine. Embed the design by rolling it through the machine. Assign the Cricut Maker's debossing tip to the design's lines and let the machine deboss the pattern.
- Remove the embossed or debossed material from the machine or folder carefully. Raised (embossed) or pressed (debossed) designs are tactile and attractive.

Exquisite Paper Cut Design

Materials:

- SVG or intricate papercutting designs
- With a fine-point blade, the Cricut Cutting Machine
- Cardstock in various colors
- Tape Transfer

Steps:

- Create or download intricate SVG paper cutting designs. These patterns are delicate and detailed.
- Upload SVG files to Cricut Design Space. Adjust element sizes and colors as needed. Cut intricate designs on the cutting mat with the right cardstock color.
- Weed (Optional): Use weeding tools to carefully remove excess paper from small design pieces.
- Carefully layer the intricate pieces to create a multi-dimensional effect. Precision glue application with a fine-tip applicator.
- Transfer tape can be used to lift and transfer the assembled paper cutting design onto the desired surface if the design is too delicate to handle directly.

Customizing 3D Objects

Materials:

- Wooden, glass, or ornamental 3D objects
- Infusible Ink or Permanent Vinyl Transfer Sheets
- With a fine-point blade, the Cricut Cutting Machine
- Weeding tools
- Transfer Tape Vinyl

Steps:

- Design: Create or choose Cricut Design Space designs for the 3D object's shape and size.
- Permanent vinyl or Infusible Ink Transfer Sheets: Cut designs. Weed out any extra material to reveal the design elements.
- Vinyl Transfer: Apply vinyl designs to the 3D object using transfer tape. Apply vinyl carefully around curves and edges to ensure smooth adhesion.
- If using Infusible Ink, cut the design mirrored and transfer it to the object using a Heat Press or EasyPress machine, according to the specified temperature and time settings.
- Permanent vinyl requires firm pressing to secure the design. A clear sealant can protect vinyl from wear and tear.

Advanced Painting Stencils:

Materials

- Mylar or stencils
- With a fine-point blade, the Cricut Cutting Machine
- Spray or acrylic paint
- To secure the stencil, use brushes or spray adhesive.

Steps:

- Design your stencil in Cricut Design Space. Maintain line continuity for structural integrity.
- Using your Cricut machine, cut the stencil material on the cutting mat.
- Secure: Brush or spray adhesive the stencil to the surface to paint.
- Paint the stencil evenly with acrylic or spray paint. Layer colors and layers for intricate designs.
- Remove: Avoid smudging by carefully removing the stencil while the paint is wet. Thoroughly dry the paint before handling.

Making Intricate Papercut Lampshades:

Materials:

- Paper Cut Lampshade Design Files Are Intricate
- Cutting machine Cricut with fine-point blade Vellum or heavyweight paper in various colors
- Glue or double-sided tape LED string lights or lamp base

Steps:

- Design: Create or download intricate SVG paper cut lampshade designs.
- Upload SVG files to Cricut Design Space. Customize size and colors. Cut the designs from vellum or heavy paper.
- Layer the paper cut pieces to create a 3D effect. Apply glue or double-sided tape to layers.
- Attach Lights: Within the papercut design, attach LED string lights for hanging lampshades. Attach a table lampshade to the lamp base after assembly.

Sewing Fabric Appliqués:

Materials:

- Multicolored fabric
- Fabric adhesive or Heat-n-Bond
- With a fine-point blade, the Cricut Cutting Machine
- Sewing machine and thread

Steps:

- Iron fabric to remove wrinkles. Apply Heat-n-Bond or fabric adhesive to fabric sheet backs.
- Design: Create appliqué shapes in Cricut Design Space.
- Cut the appliqué shapes with your Cricut machine on the prepared fabric.
- Peel and Iron: Iron fabric shapes onto the desired fabric surface after peeling off the backing.
- Use a sewing machine to permanently attach the appliqué shapes to the fabric.

Customizing Wood and Metal Home I:

Materials:

- Metal or wood sheets/items
- Permanent stencil or vinyl
- With a fine-point blade, the Cricut Cutting Machine
- Transfer Tape Vinyl
- Permanent markers or paint for metal

Steps:

- Design: Use Cricut Design Space to create or select wood or metal designs.
- Cut: Cut permanent vinyl or stencil designs. Weed excess.
- Vinyl Transfer Tape: Apply vinyl designs to wood or metal surfaces using transfer tape. To ensure adhesion, apply pressure.
- After removing the vinyl stencil, fill in metal designs with paint or permanent markers.
- To protect and strengthen the design, seal it with a clear sealant, especially for outdoor use.

These advanced techniques let you create intricate, personalized, and professional-quality projects on various materials with your Cricut machine. Try these techniques to improve your craft and create beautiful, personalized items for yourself and others.

BOOK 11:
POTENTIAL ISSUES WITH HARDWARE AND SOFTWARE AND HOW TO FIX THEM

urely this is the time to ensure that your investment is properly looked after? With everyone cutting vinyl, glitter paper, cardstock, and other products, our Cricut Explore machines tend to get a little messy. Finally, there are a few tips you should follow to maintain the cleanliness and beauty of your Cricut Explore.

Tearing or incomplete cutting of the material

The main issue that most Cricut users have is this. When this occurs, you've wasted material and damaged the image. This issue has led to the return or packaging and storage of more machines than any other.

Don't panic, though. You can fix the issue in multiple steps if your paper isn't cutting correctly. The most important thing to remember is to turn off your machine every time you work with a blade. I understand that, when you're frustrated and attempting various solutions to get it to function properly, it's simple to forget this. It is crucial that you keep in mind this safety measure. Start with minor adjustments. Decrease the pressure by one. Did it assist? Turn the blade down one number if necessary. For the blade to ride smoothly, make sure the mat is clear of debris.

Generally speaking, a higher pressure number needs to be used to cut through paper the thicker the material. Remember to utilize the multi-cut feature if available. Cutting two, three, or four times might take a little longer, but by that point, it should cut through cleanly.

Here's how to get your multi-cut to work if you're using one of the smaller bugs without that option. Don't remove the image from the mat after it has been cut. To load paper, simply click, repeat last, and cut. To make sure the entire image is cut out, you can repeat this process two, three, or four times.

Try lowering the pressure and slowing down the speed if you are using thinner paper and it is tearing. You must give the blade enough time to work its way through intricate designs when cutting them. It can make cleaner cuts by slowing down.

Make sure the blade's edge is free of fuzz, glue, and paper remnants by giving it a thorough cleaning.

Verify that the blade is installed properly. Be sure it is securely seated by taking it out and putting it back. When cutting, the blade should remain steady. It's either not installed properly or there's a problem with the blade housing if it makes a shaky movement.

Note that thicker material can be cut with a deep-cutting blade. While cutting thick card stock, you should use this blade instead. Additionally, this will keep your regular blade from wearing out. Cutting a lot of thick material will wear out your blade more quickly than cutting thinner material, requiring more frequent replacements.

Freezing of Machine

Always remember to switch out the cartridges on your machine by turning it off. It's known as "hot-swapping," and it can cause the machine to freeze from time to time when you swap out cartridges while it's still running. This seems to be more of a problem with the older models than with Expression 2.

Give your machine a rest for five or ten minutes every hour; you know how finicky electronic devices can be. Your machine may overheat and freeze if you use it for extended periods of time.

After turning off the machine, take a rest. It should work just fine if you restart it when you get back. Then, keep in mind to take your time programming the machine and to occasionally give it a break.

Avoid rapidly pressing a lengthy list of commands. It will become confused and freeze up if you give it too much information too quickly. Consider breaking up your words into multiple cuts rather than typing in one lengthy sentence. Make sure to press the special feature key first before choosing the letters if you're using them.

Power Issues

The power adapter may be the issue if you turn on your machine but nothing happens. To make sure the power cord is securely attached, jiggle it at the outlet and the machine connection. Ideally, before purchasing a new adapter, you should test the current one. See if the problem is resolved by exchanging cards with a friend. You can find replacement adapters by searching for "Cricut adapter power supply" on eBay. Here is how to test the connection points of the machine, which may also be a problem. To turn on the machine, hold down the plug where it goes into the back. The connection points will need to be soldered again if it starts to power up, which indicates that the problem is inside the machine.

Try a hard reset if the machine power comes on but won't cut. You can find detailed instructions on how to reset your machine in the resource area.

Here are some pointers specifically for users of the Cricut Expression 2. Have you turned on your machine, heard it start up, and seen it light up, but nothing happens when you try to cut? Alternatively, the LCD screen is unresponsive, or you're stuck on the welcome screen.

Here are two easy fixes you can try to recalibrate your die cutter, try a hard reset first, sometimes known as the "Rainbow Screen Reset." You'll have to go back and adjust the settings if that doesn't fix the problem.

Attempt to keep your machine updated to help cut down on errors. A message urging you to install the latest test version should appear when an update is available.

If you use third-party software that isn't compatible with the Cricut anymore, you are probably already aware that updating your machine may make the software inoperable.

If your Cricut Expression 2 shuts down while cutting heavy paper, try using the multi-cut feature and returning to the standard paper setting.

The carriage is immobile.

Check to see if the belt has broken or the car has fallen off the track if the carriage assembly does not move. That's crazy, but Provo Craft doesn't sell replacement parts. Try finding a belt that works at a vacuum repair shop.

Removing the plastic cover will reveal a small screw by the wheel that needs to be unscrewed if the wheels have fallen off the track. The wheel should now be able to be moved back onto the path.

Having Issues Getting on Your Computer

Every Cricut machine includes a USB cord that you can use to connect the machine to your computer and utilize other products such as the Cricut Gypsy, Cricut Craft Room, and Design Studio software.

Check your USB connection twice, then try a different port.

To see if a firewall or antivirus program may be preventing the connection, check your computer.

Verify that you are using the most recent firmware by performing a firmware test. There may be a need to update. While the newer machines (Expression 2, Imagine, and Gypsy) update via the Sync program, the older machines (Personal Cutter, Expression, Create, and Cake) update via firmware.

BOOK 12:
MAKING MONEY WITH CRICUT

With your innovative ideas and newly acquired skills, you could help design and build your business. There are a few problems that eager amateurs may run into, like any commencement entity, there are important questions that must be addressed in order to overcome potential obstacles. It is crucial, for instance, to discuss issues such as identifying our customer base, potential problems, alternative ways to find them, and how to turn a profit on sales from the beginning. To put it another way, it's important to begin with a strong and effective business strategy.

Industry Range

You should look into a unique platform to monetize your items, either by searching for ways to enter the global market directly or electronically. Second, since increasing sales as effectively as possible is the goal, it is preferable to focus resources on a single solution. The goal of optimizing gain and using it to expand the company should never be overlooked. As a result, the more money you raise, the more likely it is that you will invest in new techniques or materials, which will increase job performance in turn. Your business model measures your progress.

From one company to another, you will explore the possibility of shipping the items. The number of acquisitions and the number of transactions are both important in this framework. The hardest thing for a new Cricut-based business to succeed in is the production volume.

One benefit of having guaranteed contracted work is that you can bargain with suppliers to purchase a respectable amount. Consequently, it is difficult to find such "shining" opportunities because such agreements are susceptible to market forces. As a new business, you can now begin marketing your products to business customers directly.

A concept work schedule offers helpful components while businesses constantly search for creativity and quality materials. The industry is meant to serve as a hub for new connections by developing these kinds of relationships, creating more chances for upselling. The fierce competition makes it difficult to get a role, it is important to note!

From "business to customer" is another strategy for selling products. The goal of this system is to introduce your products to retail customers interested in purchasing, even though the number of products sold is very important. Imagination, creativity, or the type of medium and style you choose to operate in (e.g., T-shirts, mugs) are the keys to your growth. Having to find a store space to display your products is incredibly important. A fresh start project's endeavors include witnessing multiple sites and items.

The kick cost is the lowest of all the different strategies that have been discussed thus far, so consumers would gain. Still, starting out in the industry as a growing business can be intimidating. The first step would be hearsay, followed by the production of good items at a low cost.

How to Market Products on the Web

Unless you're an expert with more experience, you can gain a lot of benefits by offering wholesale packages, educational platforms, or successful custom projects. Focusing your efforts on just one method to begin from is preferable. For example, if you are using a custom job methodology, you increase the likelihood that potential buyers will see your products when they switch to google.com to know what to look for. Portals like Amazon, Customized, and Etsy offer a broad range of platforms for offering custom design services. The release of the webpage is equally good. It's helpful to look at that strategy. It offers features like lower startup costs and access to global infrastructure, which help to pen millions and millions of buyers.

In contrast, customized retail prices seem to be less than those at the local supermarket. However, being connected to the world market means there is fierce competition, making using commodities more affordable. A component of value that should be taken into account when calculating costs is the operational expertise required for the distribution and packaging of products when shopping online.

Regardless of whether you choose a wholesale offer or wholesale market offerings, the benefits are the same as reducing the supply per produced unit. Although Amazon.com is the main platform, you can also achieve greater success if you use an internet commerce business model. This will help you assess the level of demand for the models you offer and adjust your product accordingly. We are encouraged to explore the new industry even by investing electronically!

If you wish to expand your business digitally through an information network, you may eventually become an expert in the field. Opportunity to benefit from your Cricut ideas. You continue to exercise caution when it comes to your professional expertise or attracting employment for the posts you would only like to accept by having articles. When starting a new company, a strategic plan ought to be part of the framework in addition to your ongoing growth. What other products can you offer to everyone, or how would buyers become the first steps of a new venture, when considering where the potential is?

CONCLUSION

The Cricut Machine is a well-known invention. This product was useful for many people, not just scrapbookers, who needed it for different reasons.

We are entering a new era as we complete our profound creative journey. A time when innovation and artistry coexist, precision and passion dance, and imagination soars. The discovery of Cricut's complex world has shown human ingenuity's endless supply.

These pages cover fashion, design, sustainability, collaboration, and creativity democratization. Our silent hero, Cricut, has unleashed our creativity. As we write these final words, we consider our journey and Cricut's creative transformation.

As we finish this exploration, we realize Cricut's magic: precision. Precision goes beyond accuracy to create masterpieces from ordinary materials. Technological innovation can be a brushstroke, a sculpture, or a carefully crafted garment, as Cricut cuts show. Cricut lets designers realize their ideas in stunning detail.

Cricut is shaping couture in the ever-changing fashion world. Cricut has changed the design process from concept to creation by letting designers experiment. The machine quickly prototypes ideas, adds intricate embellishments, and turns fabrics into art, changing the industry. Cricut makes fashion a language, self-expression, and celebration of individuality.

Cricut effortlessly embodies sustainability throughout this journey. Cricut promotes upcycling and reduces fabric waste, demonstrating ethical craftsmanship. Reduces carbon emissions and promotes mindful consumption. Cricut's innovations create a greener, more sustainable, beautiful fashion future.

Cricut brings creative minds together to create gems. Cricut's precision partnerships have produced innovative products. Designers and artisans use their unique perspectives to create narratives that push artistic boundaries. Through collaboration, Cricut has promoted cultural dialogue and global creativity.

Many DIYers are inspired by Cricut. The intuitive interface and unmatched precision have democratized creativity for all ages and backgrounds. Innovation in everyday homes inspires limitless creativity. Every dreamer can create with Cricut, showcasing imagination.

BONUS

Bonus 1

Bonus 2

Bonus 3

Bonus 4

Made in United States
Troutdale, OR
02/06/2024

17495274R00075